Advance Praise for
Beyond the Sales Process

"You can sit back and wait for the next RFP, or you can read *Beyond the Sales Process* and join the next generation of highly effective B2B sales professionals. Armed with the twelve proven strategies in this book, you'll engage customers on a whole new level while creating and winning your own next opportunity."

Paul Merrild, Senior Vice President,
Enterprise Sales, athenahealth

"Creating high-value, ongoing client success begins long before the sale happens and continues long after the sale concludes. In *Beyond the Sales Process*, Steve Andersen and Dave Stein provide a clear roadmap on how to move into the high-value space of client collaboration, innovation, and mutual value creation."

Rosemary Heneghan, Director,
International Sales Organization, IBM Corporation

"*Beyond the Sales Process* details how to capture, consolidate, and then multiply the power of marketing, sales, and customer service to drive value for customers before, during, and after they buy. The Engage/Win/Grow process provides the reader with a precise approach for how to do this in today's challenging business environment."

Dr. Kourosh Bahrami, Corporate Vice President/Global Head of
Marketing and Sales/Automotive, Metal & Aerospace, Henkel

"It's easy to *say* that trust is critically important to your customer relationships—but the proof is in the doing. *Beyond the Sales Process* lays out in very practical terms *how to make it happen*: from establishing trust and credibility before there's a sales opportunity on the horizon, to helping customers solve their business problems, to growing with your customer after closing the sale, and everything in between. A must-buy.

Charles H. Green, co-author of
***The Trusted Advisor*, author of *Trust-based Selling*,**
and founder/CEO of Trusted Advisor Associates, LLC

"Most sales books assume that only the sale matters. Not true. This book considers the whole picture—what's happening when your customers *aren't* buying from you influences them when they are. Dave and Steve equip you with the right strategies to engage your customers and decisively defeat your competitors."

Yvonne Genovese, GVP, Gartner, Inc.

"Steve Andersen and Dave Stein's Engage/Win/Grow approach is profoundly compelling. . . . These two experts prove once and for all that relationships are critical to your sales success."

Craig Lemasters, President and CEO, Assurant Solutions

"If you want to learn how to win business by engaging with your customers differently than any of your competitors, Andersen and Stein lay out all the answers you'll need, and then some. The book's twelve actionable strategies and behind-the-scenes case studies offer more than just another methodology; they deliver a no-nonsense platform that will lead you directly to your next win."

Paul Nolan, Editor, *Sales & Marketing Management* magazine

Beyond the
Sales Process

12 Proven Strategies for
a Customer-Driven World

STEVE ANDERSEN and DAVE STEIN

American Management Association
New York • Atlanta • Brussels • Chicago • Mexico City
San Francisco • Shanghai • Tokyo • Toronto • Washington, D.C.

Bulk discounts available. For details visit:
www.amacombooks.org/go/specialsales
Or contact special sales:
Phone: 800-250-5308
Email: specialsls@amanet.org
View all the AMACOM titles at: www.amacombooks.org
American Management Association: www.amanet.org

Library of Congress Cataloging-in-Publication Data

Names: Andersen, Steve (Stephen S.), 1952– author. | Stein, Dave, 1947– author.
Title: Beyond the sales process : 12 proven strategies for a customer-driven world /
    Steve Andersen and Dave Stein.
Description: New York : American Management Association, [2016] | Includes bibliographical
    references and index.
Identifiers: LCCN 2015037213| ISBN 9780814437155 (hardcover) | ISBN 9780814437162
    (ebook)
Subjects: LCSH: Sales management. | Customer relations.
Classification: LCC HF5438.4 .A495 2016 | DDC 658.8/02—dc23 LC record available at
    http://lccn.loc.gov/2015037213

About AMA
American Management Association (www.amanet.org) is a world leader in talent development, advancing the skills of individuals to drive business success. Our mission is to support the goals of individuals and organizations through a complete range of products and services, including classroom and virtual seminars, webcasts, webinars, podcasts, conferences, corporate and government solutions, business books, and research. AMA's approach to improving performance combines experiential learning—learning through doing—with opportunities for ongoing professional growth at every step of one's career journey.

Printing number

10 9 8 7 6 5 4 3 2

Steve Andersen:
For Connie, Ian, Courtney, and Jason

Dave Stein:
For Vivian, Jessica, and Robyn

Contents

Acknowledgments

Steve Andersen

My contributions to this book are the result of the work that Performance Methods, Inc. (PMI) has undertaken with our clients over the past 16 years. Without the reality of these experiences, there would have been little for me to write about, and I am forever indebted to our clients for all that they have taught me and my PMI colleagues about value creation and the significance of enduring, trust-based customer relationships. The profound impact of our work with them and with their customers is evident herein.

I want to thank the Strategic Account Management Association (SAMA) for all that it continues to mean to me and to PMI. It has been my great pleasure to get to know many of the remarkable practitioners that comprise this community of practice, as well as SAMA's dedicated staff who work tirelessly to support us. The SAMA team creates compelling value for the membership, and I would specifically like to thank Bernard Quancard, Elizabeth Cornell, Brett Middendorf, Aimee Waddell, Jennifer Weed, and Nicolas Zimmerman for their encouragement, support, and contributions to our work and publications over the years.

It is my privilege to acknowledge and thank Craig Jones, who began the PMI journey with me sixteen years ago, for his ongoing role in our business and the work he does with clients—both have profoundly influenced this book. Craig's partnership, thought leadership, and ongoing encouragement were constant throughout the writing process.

Over the years, many clients and people have shaped my thinking about the evolution of customer engagement, and I owe each one a debt of gratitude. In addition to my heartfelt appreciation for the individuals and organizations that graciously agreed to directly participate in *Beyond the Sales Process,* I'd like to send out a special "thank you" to all of those who supported Dave's and my efforts through the development of the case studies. These in-depth accounts required a significant investment of time and energy from many people, and we deeply appreciate your commitment to the book and its message.

Thanks also to Doug Harward, Ken Taylor, and the TrainingIndustry.com team for the recognition and support that you have provided over the years, and to all of the salespeople, account managers, sales managers, and leaders that I have had the pleasure of working with throughout my career. I've learned much from you, and I can only hope that you learned at least a little something from me.

Finally, two special acknowledgements:

To Zack D. Andersen, father, sales professional, and the person who taught me the importance of belief, determination, and doing the right thing. He also tried to teach me patience.

To Connie Andersen, my incredible wife and life partner. Without her support, encouragement, patience, and love, my contributions to *Beyond the Sales Process* would not have been possible.

Dave Stein

My first book, *How Winners Sell,* was a professional milestone for me. Its success validated my expertise in B2B sales and propelled me into consulting with, training for, and speaking to a broader spectrum of companies than I ever had previously. In that first book, as well as the second edition published two years later, I acknowledged the people who had motivated, guided, inspired, and assisted me in reaching that pivotal point in my career.

In preparing for and working on *Beyond the Sales Process,* I have had the good fortune to add some additional direct and indirect supporters to the list, and I am delighted to acknowledge the contributions they have made:

Paul O'Dea has been a friend, trusted advisor, and colleague since 2002, when I delivered a keynote speech for Enterprise Ireland in Dublin, Ireland. Paul is one of the smartest and most successful people I know. Thanks, Paul—for your ear, your experience, and your willingness to sponsor and support this American in your country.

Paul Nolan, the Editor-in-Chief of *Sales and Marketing Management* magazine and I go way back. We became acquainted long before he assigned me the regular sales training column in the magazine. Now at the top of his game, Paul continues to encourage my efforts to educate and inform. Thanks, Paul, for being such a great supporter and an asset to our industry.

Even though I already had two books under my belt, inside sales expert and author Josiane Feigon provided friendship, advice, and insights when Steve and I were in the early stages of this journey. Thanks, Josiane.

I've worked with hundreds of clients, but in recent years, several executives stand out for being true partners—together we have co-created real business value: Thank you, Von Petersen, Kristi Fox, Cambra Aasen, Andrew Fleury, John Harrington, and Barry Cronin.

I met Claire McBride during my early days delivering programs for Enterprise Ireland, and she has remained a colleague and friend to me. Ever interested and supportive of my efforts, Claire truly knows what it means to under-promise and over-deliver.

If B2B selling has a pinnacle of integrity, Charles Green is perched at the very top. Thank you, Charlie, for being someone I genuinely trust.

Gary VanAntwerp and Philip Rodriguez are champions of my Executive Webinar Series for SMMConnect.com. Thank you, Gary and Philip, for giving me the privilege of interviewing some of the smartest people in the B2B selling and marketing world.

Thanks to Tom Martin, one of my most trusted advisors.

As my amazing and inspiring yoga instructor for many years, Bonnie Menton has had a very dramatic and positive influence on my mind, my body, and the way I look at life.

Thank you, Stanislav Saling, for your sincere interest and encouragement.

Thanks to my HOLBs.

Finally, I want to thank my wife, Vivian, for the loving support she has generously and consistently provided to me through all the years we've been together, and then some.

Steve Andersen and Dave Stein

Authors Steve Andersen and Dave Stein would like to thank the following individuals and organizations for their generous contributions of time, effort, and thought leadership to *Beyond the Sales Process:*

First and foremost, we want to thank our development editor Jennifer Bohanan. Without her, this book would likely never have been written. Jennifer is tireless, clever, knowledgeable, persistent, loyal, and a pleasure to work with. She made the authors' toils and triumphs her own, and was with us literally every step along the way from concept through publication.

Although he is now formally retired from AMACOM, Bob Nirkind's guidance, firmness, and belief in us helped us craft the type of book we initially set out to write. A sincere and well-deserved thanks, Bob.

Laura Menza is the talented, responsive, and creative graphic artist who rendered the figures in this book, working from a variety of slides, sketches, and ideas developed by the authors. We are truly thankful for her commitment to deliver on a very tight schedule, as well as for the fine quality of her work.

We appreciate the determination and effectiveness of the team at PMI: whose thought leadership, collaborative ethic, and innovation have profoundly shaped our approaches to customer engagement. Additionally, special thanks go out to Craig Jones, David Adams, Ian Andersen, Courtland Clarkson, Libby Souder, Elizabeth Strong, and Allen Tuthill for the numerous contributions they made, especially to the case studies. They came through time and time again, helping us to meet our deadlines and make it all happen.

We want to express our sincere gratitude to the individuals—some are mentioned by name; others worked behind the scenes—from the companies that contributed time and effort to the case studies contained in this book: Adecco S.A., BNY Mellon, Cargill, Inc., Dow Chemical Company, Hilton Worldwide, Honeywell Building Solutions, Merck/MSD, Panasonic Corporation, Premier, Inc., Procter & Gamble, Securian Insurance Group—Group Insurance, Siemens AG, Stora Enso, Streamlight, Inc., The University of Notre Dame, and Zurich Insurance Group.

We would like to thank Mercuri International for supporting this book and give special recognition to Henk van de Kuijt, Dave Cusdin, and Robert Box for their contributions and partnership throughout the development process.

A number of industry thought-leaders and subject matter experts contributed directly to the book or were supportive of our efforts. Our deepest appreciation goes out to Maureen Blandford, Jonathan Farrington (Top Sales World), Gerhard Gschwandtner (*Selling Power* magazine), Geoffrey James (Inc.com), Robert Kelly (Sales Management Association), Mike Kunkle (Brainshark), Dave Munn and Julie Schwartz (ITSMA), Jim Ninivaggi (SiriusDecisions), Peter Ostrow (Aberdeen Group), and Bernard Quancard (SAMA). They add significant value to our profession, and we are grateful for the value they have added to our book.

And last, but certainly not least, thanks to Stephen S. Power, Senior Editor, and everyone at Amacom who encouraged and assisted us along the way. Also, many thanks to Barbara A. Chernow and her staff at Chernow Editorial Services, Inc. It takes a team to produce a book and all of these folks are certainly part of ours.

Introduction: Why Read *Beyond the Sales Process?*

ASK A CEO to name his or her organization's most important asset and you're sure to hear "our people," followed closely by "our customers." Everything else takes a backseat, and yet few books are written about how these two most valuable assets interact, engage, align, collaborate, innovate, and create value together.

Much has been written about sales, much has been written about marketing, and much has been written about customer service. But we see remarkably little about how the world's top companies are going beyond the sales process and leveraging proven strategies *before*, *during*, and *after* the sale—not just when the customer is buying, which is where the majority of sales books tend to focus. Perhaps this is because, in order to write such a book, you must gain entry into the actual companies and their customers, and that's not easy to do. Or perhaps it's because, on the supply side, we have historically had such a one-dimensional focus on the sale that there hasn't been much appetite left for when the customer isn't buying, which is most of the time. Or perhaps it's because so much of what is currently being written about sales is being produced by those whose approaches are new and unproven, or were hatched as far back as the 1970s.

Whatever the reason, one thing is certain: business-to-business (B2B) commerce has changed dramatically in the last decade, and there's no going back. Basing your customer engagement and sales best practices on yesterday's approaches simply doesn't work any more. Top-performing salespeople and account managers have learned that in order to be successful, new and more holistic approaches are required for engaging effectively with customers, developing and winning new opportunities, and growing and sustaining their customer relationships before and after each sale.

Beyond the Sales Process focuses on the frontline of engagement with customers. It is specifically intended for salespeople, account managers, their managers, and sales leaders, as well as others who have responsibilities and pressures associated with developing and winning business, and those who are tasked with extending and expanding their relationships with customers. In the case studies that follow each section, you'll learn how top companies engage differently and grow successful customer relationships based on collaboration, innovation, and mutual value creation and co-creation. These case studies provide an in-depth perspective on how industry leaders across the globe engage, win, and grow with their customers. Adecco Staffing U.S., BNY Mellon, Hilton Worldwide, Honeywell Building Solutions, Merck/MSD, Panasonic Corporation, Securian Financial Group—Group Insurance, Siemens AG, and Zurich Insurance Group have generously provided us with their stories.

While this book is largely intended for those who want to consistently be at the top of their professional peer groups and are willing to consider new ideas to help them succeed, it will also be of value to the managers and leaders who motivate, coach, and support the efforts of their teams. Thus, this book is for those customer-facing professionals who need to drive their performance to the next level of effectiveness.

Before, During, and After the Sale

Take a moment to think about the success you hope to achieve over the next 12 months. Identify a customer that you believe will significantly impact your results. Choose wisely, because you will reflect on this customer many times as you "try on" the concepts, best practices, and tools that this book offers. Also think about your network of personal relationships within this customer organization and identify someone who is involved and invested in doing business with you. Once you have selected your customer and your individual contact, you're ready to move forward.

Most of us consider the length of a typical work year to be about fifty 40-hour workweeks, excluding vacation and holidays, which totals about 2,000 hours. With this in mind, think about your customer and consider this question: What percentage of the customer's total work time is spent actively buying from you? Here are some potential responses:

A. 25 percent (500 hours/year)

B. 10 percent (200 hours/year)

C. 2 percent (40 hours/year)

D. 1 percent (20 hours/year)

What percentage most closely matches your actual experience with your customer?

We've asked this question many times, and found that the responses are nearly always C and D. Why? *Because even when you have a successful relationship, it is likely that your customer spends less than 2 percent of their time (only 40 hours per year!) actively buying from you.* In other words, your mindshare with your customer is minuscule compared to how they spend the vast majority of their time. Unless you change this, your odds of becoming important or strategic to your customer are virtually nonexistent.

Your customer doesn't care about your sales training, sales tips, sales forms, sales processes, sales strategies, sales plans, or your sales quota attainment, because that's not what's important to them. Yet far too many salespeople and account managers expect their sales tools and techniques to miraculously win business for them, when the real problem is that they only show up when the customer announces an intention to buy. How can you expect your customer to respond favorably to you when you've been out of sight and out of mind?

In this book, we demonstrate that when you pay careful attention to the other 98 percent of your customer's time, you become strongly positioned to impact that highly leverageable 2 percent—when they're actively buying.

By interviewing many of the world's most successful salespeople and account managers and capturing the best practices of these top performers, we offer a proven approach to engaging with customers that spans the entire relationship. Customers today want more effective engagement with their most important suppliers. This book provides proven strategies and tools for determining what you need to do and instructive examples of how to do it.

How This Book Is Organized

This book is divided into three sections that document twelve proven strategies that top performers use to drive success before, during, and after the sale. The *Engage/Win/Grow* model (Figure Intro-1) will be your guide as you advance through this approach, and the case studies that follow each section will validate what we have presented. Coaching questions at the

Figure Intro-1. Beyond the Sales Process: Twelve Proven Strategies for a Customer-Driven World.

end of each strategy will help you assess your progress and effectiveness along the way.

What Matters Most to Customers

If you talk with enough customers (and we have), you realize that the things that are important to them today are vastly different from what many organizations and the people who sell and market to them seem to think they are. Customers expect more, and they deserve it. We've asked some of the world's most successful companies what their customers expect in terms of value, alignment, relationships, and growth. Their responses are consistent, profound, and decisively contradict the assertions that customer relationships are no longer important.

Customers don't want to be coerced, controlled, or otherwise pushed around. They value authentic relationships based on transparency, competence, credibility, and trust, and they'll pay more for these qualities, even in today's difficult selling environment. We've asked hundreds of customers about their experiences with vendors, suppliers, and partners, and their feedback provides a compelling case for stronger alignment, collaboration, innovation, and mutual value creation in this exciting new era of customer engagement.

It's time for a change of mindset, a change of attitude, and a change of heart regarding how sellers and buyers engage and do business together. If you're interested in reaching the next level of success in our customer-driven world, this book is for you.

I

Engage: Driving Success Before the Sale

STRATEGY 1

Research the Organization: Becoming a Student of Your Customer

WITH YOUR CUSTOMER in mind, it's time to plunge into *Engage/Win/ Grow*. You may be surprised to learn that it begins in a sparsely populated area known as the *pre-opportunity* phase, before a potential sale has even started to take shape. In this phase, you're not responding or reacting to a formal request for information about a product or service to fulfill a specific need, because no one is buying at the moment. You're simply doing some homework, and the subject area is your customer, or a prospective customer, if you haven't done business together before.

Pre-opportunity is when many salespeople and account managers don't pay attention to their customers. That's a mistake, because it's one of the few times when customers aren't feeling pressured to buy. Their wall of resistance is down, which means you're in an ideal environment to engage with them on a range of topics that they care about, without the urgency of a deadline or the limitations imposed by specific requirements. Before you think about having that conversation, however, you must first *become a student of your customer* by extending and expanding what you may already know about their business and the forces affecting their world. You accomplish this through research.

Like a surfer paddling out past the breakers, you're looking to catch a wave. And even if you can't see that wave—an opportunity—on the horizon, there's almost certainly one coming. If you don't prepare in advance, you'll miss it just like everyone else who isn't paying attention. Becoming a student of your customer and their industry equips you with the knowledge you need to get ahead of the curve and, as you do so, leave your competitors behind.

At this moment, an undefined opportunity may seem too distant to concern yourself with, but at the speed business operates today, you won't have much time to collect information and develop knowledge once an opportunity arrives. If you've researched and done your homework, you'll be in a stronger position to compete. Becoming a student of your customer makes all the sense in the world if you want to engage, win, and grow with them. But be advised: if it were easy, every salesperson would do it, and they don't. Why? Because it isn't free, and, in fact, it's rather expensive. To become a student of your customer, you'll have to make a substantial investment of what you probably consider to be a most precious asset: your time.

Coauthor Steve Andersen once heard an account manager make a comment that seems counterintuitive: "I do my best selling when my customer isn't buying." Steve asked her to explain. "When they're buying, everything is different," she responded. "The walls are up. There's pressure, there's stress, and the people in my customer's organization behave differently. When the customer isn't buying, I can take steps to distinguish myself and my organization, and they're much more open with me."

The best time to become a student of your customer is *before the sale*, when the next opportunity is just a flicker out on the horizon, if visible at all. This will require an investment of your time—but the return can be huge. The payoff for doing your research, completing your homework, and studying your customer, their business, and their industry is no less than your future success, as you catch sight of that wave in the distance and begin to set yourself up to engage more effectively with your customer.

What You Need to Know About Your Customer

If you were that surfer looking to catch the perfect wave, you would want to do some research before stepping into the ocean. You'd check the weather, tides, wave conditions, and water temperature. You'd test your equipment, and make sure you're stocked up on wax. Only after you'd collected all the relevant information would you throw your board on your car's roof rack and head to the beach.

Likewise, as a student of your customer, you have information to gather before you're ready to engage with them. This requires you to focus your efforts on asking good questions, and refraining from early temptations to position what you are able to do for their organization. Your customer is not ready to hear it yet, because they aren't buying anything at the moment.

As Figure 1-1 illustrates, you'll need a variety of information to begin to build a solid foundation upon which to engage your customer.

As you review the twelve categories we discuss here, keep in mind that some may seem critically important and others less so. Your goal is to avoid finding out later that you didn't research something that you should have.

Your Customer's Organization. *How is your customer structured to do business?* We've witnessed too many salespeople and account managers

---

UNDERSTAND YOUR CUSTOMER

▷ Their organization
▷ Their news and developments
▷ Their culture
▷ Their industry
▷ Their drivers, objectives, and challenges
▷ Their value proposition

▷ Their customers
▷ Their partners
▷ Their competitors
▷ Their buying and decision processes
▷ Their people
▷ Their history (with you)

Figure 1-1. **Understand your customer.**

spending far too much time drafting highly detailed organization charts, trying to identify who's responsible for what in their customer's organization, and not gaining much value from the exercise. Yes, you do need to know about your customer's organizational hierarchy, but be prepared for it to change. Rather than tinkering endlessly with the latest organization chart software, it might be more helpful to focus on how your customer is structured to do business (subsidiaries and business units), where they do business, and the type of global organization (regions, countries, etc.) they have in place.

Your Customer's News and Developments. *What's happening in your customer's world? What internal or external events could trigger a new initiative on which you might make a positive impact?* In the Internet age, there's no excuse for lagging behind in knowing what's happening with and around your customer's business. Just a few years ago, you could walk into a meeting and be blindsided by unexpected news, but those days are gone and they're not coming back. Even at the last minute before a meeting, you can do a quick Internet search to make sure you're up-to-date on any news, developments, and recent events regarding your customer's business. You should never enter a customer meeting without checking last-minute news and developments.

Your Customer's Culture. *What is it like to do business with your customer?* Learning what you can about your customer's organizational values, attitudes, standards, behaviors, and beliefs can empower your efforts to build value-focused relationships with the organization's team members. This will become vitally important when they start to think about buying. Are team members open about information? Do they collaborate with suppliers? Are they innovative?

If you forge ahead without understanding your customer's culture, you risk doing or saying something insensitive, and possibly communicating, albeit inadvertently, that you're not in philosophical alignment with them. It's fair to say that this can damage your credibility and prevent you from ever getting out of the "starting blocks" with that organization.

Fortunately, social media and other technologies can streamline your ability to learn about your customer's culture, as well as a variety of other aspects of who they are and how they operate.

Your Customer's Industry. *How is your customer viewed within its industry?* Most industries have leaders and laggards, top performers and underachievers, and it's important to understand how your customer is regarded by its peers, competitors, customers, and suppliers.

This book features nine case studies of industry leaders from across the globe with indisputable reputations for excellence in such industries as financial services, pharmaceuticals, hospitality, insurance, manufacturing, and staffing. In what industry or industries does your customer participate? How is your customer perceived by those familiar with how they operate? You can also learn a great deal about an organization by following what industry analysts say (or don't say) about them.

Your Customer's Drivers, Objectives, and Challenges. *What market factors and pressures could compel your customer to take action? External drivers* are the pressures outside of your customer's control that they must respond to, or that are causing them to change. *Business objectives* are your customer's planned responses to those external drivers, or how they intend to react to the forces outside their control. *Internal challenges* are the problems and obstacles keeping your customer from attaining their business objectives, or the blocking factors and hurdles that are standing between them and success. We'll take a closer look at all three terms a bit later, but for now, you're simply beginning to familiarize yourself with what's happening in your customer's world. Your research should help you start to identify your customer's drivers, objectives, and challenges.

Your Customer's Value Propositions. *What does your customer do to create value for their customers, and to co-create value with their customers?* What types of solutions does your customer bring to market and how do they bring their solutions to market for their own customers? If your customer has a culture of value co-creation with *their* customers, they will be more likely to co-create and collaborate with you. Sometimes finding those answers can be as simple as a website review; in other instances, you'll have to dig through securities or industry analyst reports, financial statements, LinkedIn group discussions, and other readily available sources.

How does your customer position the advantages they offer? You can learn much about an organization by understanding how they position themselves within their markets, and the types of advantages they believe set them apart from their competitors.

Does your customer publish success stories? If your customer has had a success where you have had a success, this common ground can triangulate into an interesting and powerful conversation.

Your Customer's Customers. *Who are your customer's most significant customers?* If a small percentage of the organizations that do business with your customer constitute a high percentage of their revenue, it's wise to know who those customers are, particularly the largest ones. Then, when you're communicating with your customer, you're not just hypothesizing about where they do business, you actually know.

Your Customer's Partners. *Who does your customer partner with to create mutual market value?* Many organizations have a network of companies that they consider to be business partners, and in some cases they even go to market together. By understanding who your customer partners with and why, you can gain insight into their business, and perhaps even gauge their willingness to grow a relationship with you that is more partner-oriented than vendor-oriented. And, if one of their most strategic partners happens to be one of your customers, it can also make for interesting conversation, as well as provide you with a potential source of information about your customer.

Your Customer's Competitors. *Who does your customer compete with?* Does the competition vary from market to market? If your own organization is in a relationship with your customer's biggest competitor, you want to be aware of it so you can finesse your approach, if necessary. Just as importantly, if your customer's competitor is not doing business with you, then which of *your* competitors are their suppliers? Sometimes customers will like the idea that you have experience with others in their market. On the other hand, they might be more open to discussing sensitive areas of their business if you are not doing business with their competitors.

Your Customer's Buying and Decision Processes. *How does your customer typically make purchases?* Do they make decisions by committee, and are they known to issue requests for information (RFIs), followed by requests for proposals (RFPs) or invitations to tender (ITTs), followed by bidder's conferences? It's to your benefit to be aware of this in advance, as you prepare to engage with your customer before the next sale. Is their procurement localized, distributed, or controlled globally through a centralized sourcing function? Regarding contract terms and conditions, is your customer interested in an agreement that both parties can be successful with, or are they known to enter negotiations with 120-day payment terms, ownership of anything a supplier even waves in their direction, and insistence on the most favorable pricing that you have ever provided to a customer?

If you and the customer are already in a relationship, then your experience can provide you with insight about how they do business. But when you're working with a new customer, you may not fully understand their expectations in the areas of contract terms and conditions until you're sitting at the table with their negotiators.

Your Customer's People. *Who are the key people within your customer's organization?* Who sits on the board, who's in the C-suite, and who are the decision makers? Who's on the management team and how do they interact politically? Where are they geographically located and where were they previously employed? Business is so complex today that senior leaders commonly consult "down" or outside of their organizations, talking with specialists who know more about the details. Who are the "go-to" thought leaders and influencers within your customer's organization? What consultants and trusted partners from outside the organization have a current relationship and a history with your customer?

Your Customer's History. *What sort of history does your customer have with you, your organization, and your competitors?* Your customer relationship management (CRM) solution is a good place to start an exploration of your own company's history with your customer, but it won't provide you with the complete picture. What's most important is to understand your customer's history with your organization (including your predecessors and current team members), and to have a sense of their past experiences (if any) with your major competitors. A particularly bad customer experience can put you in a deep hole before an opportunity surfaces, while a significant success or creation of past proven value can have the opposite effect and provide you with early momentum.

How B2B Buyers Consume Information, a 2014 study conducted by ITSMA, a member community that helps B2B marketing organizations advance their knowledge, skills, and impact, asked buyers to rank by importance sixteen characteristics of solution providers. Tied at the top of the list were "knowledge and understanding of my unique business issues" and "knowledge and understanding of my industry." Customers clearly appreciate when a supplier has invested time and effort getting to know their world—one more good reason to become a student of your customer.

Where You Can Acquire and Capture Customer Knowledge

We've unpacked the various types of customer information you need to seek out through your research, but knowing where to turn to find it can be a challenge. And in this age of TMI (too much information), you're likely to be as overwhelmed by too much information coming at you too fast from unreliable sources as you once were by having to read every newspaper and industry publication you could find in a desperate search for information, and spending far too many hours at the library doing so. The following list of sources, while not comprehensive, will put you on track for discovering what you need to know.

Knowledge from Within Your Organization. Steve recently heard a senior executive from one of his clients lament, "If we only knew what we know!" This particular executive was referring to his relationship with a very large customer that operates through multiple business units that span the globe. Each unit has its own institutional history and knowledge, which can be difficult, if not impossible, to aggregate across the entire organization because of the scale of the business. Compound this with the difficulty that many organizations experience sharing customer information across sales and account teams, and it's easy to see why collectively "knowing what we know" is easier said than done. Steve's client is more the rule than the exception; most organizations find themselves challenged when it comes to sharing customer information internally.

When you're looking to find out what you already know, you can begin with a look at the sources that might exist within your own company.

- **Enabling technology (CRM-type applications).** Technology is not the only way to capture and access institutional history, but it is one way, and it can be a good one, when implemented properly. If you have access to this type of enabler, you should use it with no worries about it being "management spyware." The potential upside far outweighs any downside that you may be inclined to attribute to these technologies. If you've had a bad experience (and we've seen more than a few), it's almost always a function of implementation missteps, not technology inadequacies. Intranet portals and sales enablement tools can provide significant information "in the moment" if you're willing to invest some time and effort in learning how to use them—as well as making your own contributions to the base of knowledge that your company is capturing about your customer.

- **Sales and account team members.** Under pressure to perform at the speed of business, salespeople today frequently miss opportunities to collaborate with their own team members. Many clients ask for our help in deploying sales and account management best practices in customer-specific, team-centric environments. When we facilitate these workshops, we find again and again that an amazing amount of new information is shared through collaboration.

Your team members and coworkers who currently interact or have previous experience with your customer are a valuable knowledge asset that should be leveraged on an ongoing basis.

- **Stakeholders and global colleagues.** It's highly likely that you and your sales/account team members are not the only people in your organization who have history with your customer. Stakeholders in such areas as product groups, customer service, finance, and even the legal department frequently have insight into your customer through their own personal experiences. If you're in a global organization that does business with global customers, and you're not collaborating and comparing notes with global colleagues who are also invested in your customer, it's an opportunity lost.

- **Customer loyalty and satisfaction surveys.** If you've previously done business with your customer and they have completed a customer loyalty or satisfaction survey, you can use their responses to gauge how they perceived the value that your organization has provided. It's always interesting to learn how many organizations regularly gather this kind of information, and how few people actually use or even know about it. You should find out if this type of information is available to you, and if so, begin to use it.

Knowledge from Outside of Your Organization. Over the past 5 years, coauthor Dave Stein has observed a dramatic uptick in salespeople's use of Internet and social media tools for business purposes. He believes this trend will continue as the speed of business gets faster and an increasing number of professionals are seeking to better understand their customers. Here are some sources to consider when you're seeking out knowledge about your customer and their world.

- **The Internet.** The Internet offers an endless number of places to find the kind of information you want. Visit the company website, read their press releases, and explore the trade or professional associations they belong to. This is research "table stakes" and there is no excuse for not being up-to-date on what's floating around on the Internet about your most important customers. If you're not interested enough in your customer to make it your business to, at minimum, follow breaking news about them online, how can you expect them to take you seriously? (Note: As an advocate for staying current on what's going on in your customer's world, Dave has been quoted in *Forbes* about the value of Google Alerts, a very powerful—and free—tool, which too few salespeople and account managers use.)

- **Social media.** At relatively little or no cost, social media can be a rich and limitless repository for continually evolving information about your customer, giving you the ability to identify potential customers, build your company's brand (and your personal brand) into the markets you sell to, provide content that can compel your customer to seek you out for advice, and nurture relationships with existing and potential customers.

  While you can choose one or more platforms from a wide variety of social media networks, perhaps none is as easy to use and has as high an impact as LinkedIn. If you are one of the few remaining salespeople and account managers who aren't a member, it's time to join. And if you are a member who isn't leveraging the network to the fullest, it's time to get started. An enormous amount of information is available through LinkedIn, as well as Facebook, Twitter, and Google+.

  Your own online profiles should highlight the value you have delivered to customers in the past and across different positions you've held. Your personal impact with your customer will be limited if your LinkedIn profile, for example, is all about how much you've sold and what percent of target you achieved. That's the last thing customers want to know. They do want to know, however, who you are and why they should be comfortable doing business with you.

- **Marketing research.** You can find out what's being said and published about your customer's organization by doing a bit of homework. Many industries have research firms that track the activities of companies that are comparable to one another. Gartner, for example, is known for its outstanding insight on technology-related businesses. Think about who follows your customer within their industry. Does an analyst group or research firm keep tabs on your customer and similar companies, and publish related research? How can you obtain that information? Sometimes you have to buy it; sometimes it's free and accessible on the Internet. Is your customer involved with any trade, professional, or other membership organizations? Is there an annual conference or trade show that your customer attends or participates in? We mentioned analyst reports earlier, in the context of what you need to know; the point is that you have to seek this information out if you want to put it to use.

- **Your customer.** The best source for information about your customer is your customer. What do they say about themselves? If you're in an existing relationship, these are conversations that you should already be having. If you're pursuing a new customer, you'll need to determine the point at which these types of conversations are appropriate.

  Even in a new customer relationship or when you're interacting with a new contact within an existing customer relationship, you can sometimes say that you've done some homework and that you're interested in knowing more about their business. If you haven't yet earned the right to ask your customer to provide you with new information, you may be more comfortable asking them to validate or invalidate what you think you already know. It could be as simple as relating a recent press release about a new acquisition or an expansion into a new market. You can ask what it means to their business—and what it might mean to your contacts personally. Even in the earliest stages, when you're doing your research, almost anything you learn directly from the customer is likely to be helpful to you at some point in your relationship with them.

How You Can Leverage Customer Knowledge

Once you've accumulated information from as many of these sources as you can, you'll need to put it to use. Socializing or sharing information with your colleagues plays an integral role in contemporary selling; if it makes you uncomfortable, it's time to make a change. Internal collaboration is critical in helping you know what your organization knows. And when you're willing to share what you know about your customer, you may be surprised at what you get back in return.

The basic objective of your research is to develop and capture early insights about your customer. It's most likely too soon to build a case for doing something you want to do; you're simply looking for information that may become more valuable as you move ahead. The investment of your time will prepare you to engage with the customer, and it's a best practice that enables the "best of the best" salespeople and account managers to consistently outperform others.

Testing the Effectiveness of Your Research

The following six sets of questions will help you determine whether your research has been effective:

1. **What's going on in your customer's business?** Have they been in the news, and if so, why? Are they expanding or shrinking, acquiring or divesting, and if so, how? Have you checked your sources for any newsworthy developments today?

2. **How is your customer perceived within their industry?** Are they seen as a leader, and if so, why? Are they considered to be an innovator, and if so, why? Do they have a reputation for excellence, and if so, why? Are they open and collaborative with suppliers?

3. **Do you understand your customer's value proposition?** How do they create value for their customers? Are there any published customer success stories and if so, have you read them? Have you gained insights into at least some of your customer's external

drivers, business objectives, or internal challenges, and if so, what are they?

4. **Which organizations does your customer consider to be significant to their business?** Who are their key or strategic customers? Their go-to-market business partners? Their competitors?

5. **Have you identified key people within your customer's organization?** Who are the primary executives and decision makers? Thought leaders and influencers? External consultants or trusted partners?

6. **Have you reviewed your organization's history with your customer?** Is it positive? What is their history with your competitors?

STRATEGY 2

Explore the Possibilities: Giving Your Customer a Reason to Engage

IN STRATEGY 1, you became a student of your customer. Gathering information from a variety of sources, you learned about your customer's world and what's important to them. As we move into Strategy 2, you're still pre-opportunity, but it's not the time to sit back and wait for your customer to make contact with you. If you want to be distinguishable when the next opportunity arises, you have to get out ahead of the curve. You have to give your customer a reason to engage with you.

Exploring the possibilities with your customer involves initiating a dialogue to find out what your customer cares most about and identifying areas of potential interest. If you've done your research properly, you'll enter this discussion with a basic but wide-ranging knowledge of the world your customer inhabits. You're equipped to speak to your customer in a way that few, if any, of your competitors are able to, but you still have to earn the right to engage. In the exploration phase, you make use of the time and effort you've invested in research by leveraging the information you've gathered about your customer and giving them a reason to engage by demonstrating that it might be to their benefit to do so.

Initiating the Customer Dialogue

With an existing customer, it's likely that you've already achieved a level of relationship that makes it easier to initiate a conversation about what you've learned through your research. But if you're working with a new customer, you probably don't have the credibility that experience and history can provide, so you have to take a different approach. This is where your research and diligence can be particularly valuable, because it gives you the credibility to say, "I've done some research, I've learned a few things about your business, and I would like to have a conversation with you about it."

Whether it's an existing relationship or a potential new one, you have a far better chance of speaking with your customer if they feel that they have something to gain by investing their most valuable asset—their time—with you. You're about to demonstrate to them why this is, indeed, the case.

Why Should Your Customer Engage with You? According to Jim Ninivaggi, Service Director of Sales Enablement Strategies at SiriusDecisions, a 2015 study performed by this global B2B research and advisory firm asked senior sales enablement executives about their top selling challenges. Seventy-one percent responded that the number-one issue preventing their sales reps from hitting quota is their "inability to connect our offerings to the business issues of our clients," and that, as a result, their reps "can't sell the value of our offerings." This response has topped this list for the past 5 years.

One of your goals before the sale is to avoid making this mistake by standing out from the pack (your competitors), and giving your customer a reason to engage with you before there's even an opportunity for anyone to pursue. Doing your homework can be the catalyst for engagement, because you'll be able to focus on discovering what your customer really cares about. They'll believe that engaging with you is a good investment of *their* time if it's clear that you've invested *your* time in learning about them. Who knows—they might even believe that they can learn from you, or at least emerge from your discussion with a new idea or two to consider.

Based on the credibility you've earned through the diligence of your research, you and your customer are going to go exploring together. Setting out on this type of journey is a personal decision that many salespeople and account managers choose every day not to make. There's no question that waiting for your customer to reach out to you is the well-trodden, easier path, and that declining to make the journey will reduce your stress: no flights to book, luggage to lose, security lines to stand in at the airport, or parking places to search for. But when you choose to embark on the journey and embrace the opportunity to explore with your customer, you distinguish yourself. Wouldn't it be great if, among all the competitors vying for the customer's business, you're the only one who makes the decision to gain a deep knowledge of the customer—not because they're buying, but simply because you want to know more? When you're not just trying to win the opportunity at hand, your authenticity becomes clear to your customer, and they're likely to both observe and appreciate your difference. You will have distinguished yourself simply by the way that you have engaged.

Investigating What Your Customer Cares About. If you're going exploring with your customer, you're likely to be more successful if you have the heart and mind of the explorer. We've all heard about history's greatest adventurers, and we're by no means comparing their vast achievements with your intent to explore possibilities with your customers. But we think it's fair to say that true exploration requires a willing heart and an inquiring mind, lest the distractions of everyday life take precedence over even the best intentions to "stay the course."

A simple definition of an explorer might be someone who investigates places and things that are unknown. When you're a salesperson or account manager, the "unknown" includes anything that you learn about your customer that you didn't know before. When you commit yourself to exploring possibilities with your customer, you're in search of information. Notice that we don't say "in search of data," because you need more than data. You're looking for information that can lead to meaningful insights, which will evolve into a level of understanding that empowers you to take the appropriate actions on your customer's behalf. More on this later, but for now you're simply looking for information and the resulting insights that will follow.

The Essence of Exploration: Curiosity and the Inquiring Mind

In any exploration, heart is certainly important. But it's also fair to say that most great explorers would never have left their home port without a "spark" that compelled them to leave comfort behind to seek out realms unknown. For most successful sales professionals, a natural, irrepressible curiosity and an inquiring mind drive the quest for knowledge and information about their customers. The journey to gain insight can seem circuitous and daunting at the outset, but there is a strong likelihood that only one or two salespeople competing in any given account have the heart or spark to chart the uncharted course, and to invite the customer to come along. Those salespeople are the most likely to succeed at finding what they're looking for. Are you one of them?

The value of this type of exploration is not just limited to external interactions with your customer. Often, when information and insights begin to flow freely during sales/account team meetings, as well as other internal interactions and collaborations, people learn things they didn't know before. Your quest for "knowing what you know" organizationally can lead to new and sometimes surprising revelations and inspiration for everyone on your team, including you.

Steve recalls facilitating a global, cross-functional team meeting for a well-known industry leader that had convened to collaborate and build plans for an important customer. In an exercise designed to identify potential areas for exploration, two participants mentioned the same pre-opportunity situation, each having only half the "story," and both were ready to walk away none the wiser. By exploring together and pooling their respective knowledge and insights, they later won business in excess of $7 million, which they certainly would not have, had they continued working as individuals. Imagine what you can do in a room of your peers and colleagues when the spark of curiosity is lit and inquiring minds engage in customer-centric collaboration.

In a perfect world, internal collaboration takes place before you ask your customer to explore the possibilities with you. But the reality is that you will soon enough find yourself in front of your customer, whether you've had an opportunity for internal collaboration or not, and you'll need to be equipped with all of the information and insight you've managed to gather. It's up to you to do whatever you can to make this meeting successful for both parties. Your knowledge of the customer, invigorated by your curiosity and willingness to inquire, should create an ideal climate for exploration.

Timing Is Everything. Exploring the possibilities can pay dividends for you, your team members, your colleagues, and your customers, but keep in mind that timing—your customer's timing, that is—matters. Exploration needs to happen before you're responding to an RFP (or any formal request for information), because once the RFP is issued, it's too late. The best time to explore is when your customer is not buying, because the walls are down, there's nothing blocking your access, and transparency is more comfortable. When you're not trying to sell anything, your customer calculates costs in terms of their time commitment, and information-sharing exerts considerably less pressure than fielding a barrage of after-the-fact inquiries from salespeople posturing to win a specific opportunity.

Time is precious to your customer. You've got to engage them effectively so they will feel that it's worth it to engage with you at all. Your research (Strategy 1) enables you to enter the conversation informed; your exploration (Strategy 2) enables you to focus on what is most important to your customer; and your visioning (which we will discuss in Strategy 3) will position you to engage your customer effectively. Always remember that you're far better off approaching your customer at *their* right time (not yours) than you are trying to force a meeting at the wrong time, when their attention is taken up with other priorities (which can include when they are buying something). When it comes to exploring possibilities with your customer, timing is everything, and you're more likely to get their attention and focus if you're discussing the things that they care most about.

What Does Your Customer Care Most About?

Thanks to your research, you already have some initial information, and perhaps even a little insight into what your customer cares about, and where it overlaps with what you may be able to offer. Think about your personal experience as a customer—isn't it more interesting when a salesperson talks to you about something that connects to what's happening in your world rather than opening with trying to sell you something? On a personal level, we all have pressures, plans, and problems that stand in our way, and it is the pursuit of products, services, solutions, and value to address them that typically causes us to take action. Your customer is no different: they have pressures, plans, and problems, too; these are the things that they care most about.

In Strategy 1, we introduced external drivers, business objectives, and internal challenges, and later, we'll go into more detail about the key considerations that drive your customer's organization to take action. But in the context of exploration with individual members of your customer's team, the question, "What does your customer care about most?" is typically answered by recognizing the *personal* drivers that are exerting pressure on them, the *personal* objectives and plans that they are pursuing, and the *personal* challenges or problems that can prevent them from meeting their objectives and plans. When you understand these factors, you can put yourself in a much stronger position to enter into dialogue with the members of the customer's team about the things that will ultimately determine their *personal* success. This is a conversation that most customers are willing, and perhaps even eager, to have.

Based on your research and initial exploration, you're now in a more advantageous position to engage your customer. You understand what's important to them, and the types of drivers and pressures that are confronting their business. You have preliminary insight into your customer's objectives and plans and their specific role in their organization's pursuit of success. And you have identified the potential challenges and problems that could derail your customer's success, and perhaps even the impact that it could have on individual members of your customer's team with whom you are connected.

While you're now in a much stronger place than you were before, always keep in mind that there is no guarantee that your exploration will lead you to your next opportunity. You may do your research, complete your homework, and go exploring, only to be disappointed in the short term. But even if you come up empty, and your exploration doesn't pay off today, you have, at a minimum, engaged differently. And by distinguishing yourself through more effective customer engagement, you have already started to set yourself apart from other providers.

There's a much stronger likelihood that you won't be disappointed when you're an effective "customer explorer." You'll frequently find yourself in a target-rich environment as a result, which means that you may be on the verge of identifying several potentially interesting possibilities worthy of exploration, as Figure 2-1 illustrates. Your challenge now is to prioritize these possibilities with your customer to ensure that your focus is aligned with theirs. This begins by reaching back to the customer knowledge that you gained through your research and reflecting on it in the context of what seems to be most important to the people with whom you are specifically engaged. As a student of your customer, you have strengthened your ability to select the right possibilities for exploration because you understand what's most important to your customer and what the people on their team care most about. As you begin to prioritize and focus, reconsider the twelve knowledge categories covered in Strategy 1. Don't be surprised if you find that some areas overlap and intersect. Of course they do—they all have your customer in common.

Think about your customer's *organization*. How are they structured to do business and what types of changes have they experienced (mergers, acquisitions, divestitures, etc.)?

What about any recent *news and developments* that relate back to your customer? Are there good things happening? Are these difficult times for your customer? Perhaps it's both. Understanding what's happening to your

GIVE YOUR CUSTOMER A REASON TO ENGAGE

RESEARCH AREA	TO WHICH OF THESE CAN YOU ANSWER YES?
Their Organization	Can you help your customer grow it?
Their News and Developments	Can you help your customer adapt to it?
Their Culture	Can you help your customer evolve it?
Their Industry	Can you help your customer lead it?
Their Drivers, Objectives, and Challenges	Can you help your customer succeed?
Their Value Proposition	Can you help your customer expand it?
Their Customers	Can you help your customer delight them?
Their Partners	Can you help your customer create value with them?
Their Competitors	Can you help your customer defeat them?
Their Buying and Decision Processes	Can you help your customer and work within them?
Their People	Can you help your customer develop them?
Their History (with You)	Can you help your customer accrue past proven value?

Figure 2-1. Give your customer a reason to engage.

customer as reported by the media is critical, and there's simply no excuse for not being reasonably aware.

What have you heard about your customer's *culture*? Are they (or have they been) involved in any major changes or initiatives that have fundamentally transformed their business?

Think about your customer's *industry*. You've probably never heard anyone say, "I don't want to be a leader in my industry," unless, perhaps, it's the type of company that wins based purely on price. (If that's the case, industry leadership is probably not a corporate goal.) What can you do to help your customer increase their industry leadership or perceived thought leadership within their industry?

Consider your customer's *drivers, objectives, and challenges.* How might your solutions and resources help your customer succeed by meeting and exceeding their objectives? Your own organization may have the subject matter expertise to enable your customer with new best practices. Companies today place great value on suppliers that can offer expertise and best practices via expert resources.

What about your customer's *value proposition* and how they differentiate themselves from their peers? Are you able to help your customer strengthen or expand the value that they bring to market?

Most companies want loyal *customers*, and your customer will appreciate anything you can do to help them create value for the people and organizations that buy from them.

The same goes for the *partners* that your customer goes to market with. Are you able to add some of your own value to your customer's value creation efforts with their partners?

And, just like you, your customer has *competitors* that they're very interested in defeating. As you consider possibilities to explore, think about ways that you and your organization can enable your customer to be more competitive and win more business.

How does your customer do business? Can you make it easier for them to engage with your organization by aligning with their *buying and decision processes*? It's no secret that some companies are difficult to do business with, and you can look at this as either a problem or an opportunity.

What about your customer's *people*, their organization's human capital? Can you help your customer develop their staff by sharing best practices or perhaps even through training? It's not as uncommon as it may sound—when you add value to your customer's business through knowledge or skills transfer, it will bring the two organizations closer together.

Does your organization have a successful track record or *history* with the customer? If you're engaging with a new customer, then you probably haven't had an opportunity to create past proven value because the two organizations don't share any history together. But if you're engaging with an existing customer, be prepared to discuss the value that the two companies have co-created together. Too many salespeople and account managers undervalue their history with their customers. If your track record is positive, why wouldn't you want to discuss, leverage, and seek to repeat it? If it's not so positive, you'd better be the one to bring it up; it's a rare occasion when poor history or perceived supplier underperformance is not an issue going forward.

You only need one of the twelve possibilities shown in Figure 2-1 to get you started (although two or three is better). With even a few significant possibilities to explore, you'll be prepared to have a conversation with your customer that none of your competitors is able to have.

Remember this: whatever you focus on, it must be authentic, and it must be a result of your research and sincere desire to ultimately create value for your customer. If your conversation is laced with words and phrases like *deal, promotion, limited time only, special pricing, sell,* and *discount,* your customer may believe that you are only looking for an excuse to discuss your next sale. If your exploration is authentic, there should be something in it for the customer, and the customer should fully expect there to ultimately be something in it for you.

At this point, you're only asking your customer to invest a bit of time discussing several topics (you should have a preselected short list), and to be open-minded about exploring these together with you. If your customer believes you are authentic, that you have done your homework, that you are committed to explore areas of potential value to their business, and that you genuinely want to help them be successful, why wouldn't they be willing to invest time to do some exploring with you?

Are You Willing to Make the Required Investments?

More often than not, when an exploration of the possibilities with your customer hasn't occurred in advance of an opportunity, the supplier—not the customer—is to blame. We've suggested a dozen exploratory topics, and it's likely that you've identified at least one that may be important to your customer. That's all well and good, but you also have to give some thought to what can stop you from moving forward. The following questions are important to ask yourself, and if you don't take some time to answer and reflect on them, then further exploration with your customer is unlikely—you'll just have to be patient and wait for the arrival of your next RFP.

- **Are you willing to facilitate a collaborative discussion with your customer?** By now you should have an idea that you're onto something interesting, which increases the probability your conversations will eventually take you somewhere. But, because there's no guarantee that your exploratory discussions will lead to anything in terms of new opportunities for you and your organization, you have to decide whether you will invest in exploration with your customer by facilitating a collaborative discussion with them.

- **Are you willing to share best practices with your customer?** Quite candidly, the best way to motivate your customer to join you on the road to visioning (the next important strategy) is to share ideas, knowledge, and best practices with them. You may balk at that idea—why bother sharing if there's nothing in it for you? That's the half-empty view. Why wouldn't you do this if you're trying to give your customer a reason to explore possibilities with you, which will likely lead to visioning together? And what customer wouldn't want to hear how you and your organization have helped others be successful? So you have to decide whether you will make an investment with your customer by sharing ideas, knowledge, and best practices.

- **Are you willing to target areas for innovation and co-innovation with your customer?** Organizations that consider themselves to be innovative tend to be open to new ideas. As business becomes more competitive, and business cycle times spin faster and faster, you're unlikely to hear any organization or customer proclaim that they don't care to innovate, assuming they have the time and creative food-for-thought to do so. If you can offer ideas in the area of innovation that are worthy of discussion, why wouldn't your customer take you up on it? And if the customer is able to offer innovative ideas for your consideration, why wouldn't you be interested?

You may worry that you're going to identify a potential area of innovation and your customer will turn right around and hand it to one of your competitors. Yes, there's always a possibility of this happening, but that's a defensive way to do business. We believe that there's a much greater likelihood that your customer will consider your idea, look at its source (you), and decide that there's value in continuing your exploration together. You have to decide whether you will make an investment with your customer by entering into discussions of how your two organizations can innovate or perhaps even co-innovate together.

Taking Inventory of Your Assets

As you prepare to go exploring with your customer, it's wise to consider the specific assets that you may need to invest in your journey: your time, your team members, your collective talent (knowledge, skills, and abilities), and the technologies (such as CRM and social media) that are available to you. We suggest that, of all those assets, time is probably the most precious, so it's up to you to choose wisely the possibilities that you will explore.

There's a strong likelihood at this point that your customer is interested in talking about what success might look like to them, and how your organization might participate. If so, you're moving steadily closer to your next opportunity, but you have a significant decision to make. Are you going to invest your assets to support this exploration? Think carefully, because you can only explore insofar as you have the adequate time, team members, collective talent, and sales enablement technologies to do so. The decision is yours, and since you can't invest all of your resources in every potential area of exploration, you have to prioritize. But if, through your research and exploration with your customer, you've developed an understanding of what they care most about and you've given them a reason to engage, you and your customer have already begun to build a vision of success together. Now, your job is to determine if that vision of your customer's success is going to include you.

Testing the Effectiveness of Your Exploration

The following six sets of questions will help you evaluate the strength of your exploration with your customer:

1. **Is the timing right for your customer to explore possibilities with you?** Are they consumed with other priorities, and if so, when will the timing be better? Have there been any recent developments that are compelling them to consider new ideas and perhaps adjust priorities? Might they be exploring possibilities with your competitor?

2. **Have you given your customer reasons to engage and explore possibilities with you?** If so, will it ultimately translate into value for the customer's own customers and partners? What is that value? How will it ultimately translate into competitive advantage and help strengthen your customer's market position? Which of the items in Figure 2-1 are most likely to help you start the dialogue?

3. **Do you understand what success looks like to your customer?** If so, can you describe it? Have they had success with you and your organization before, and if so, what was it? Have they had success with any of your competitors, and if so, what was it?

4. **Do you understand what your customer cares most about?** Do you understand their personal drivers, and if so, what are they? Do you understand their personal objectives, and if so, what are they? Do you understand their personal challenges, and if so, what are they?

5. **Do you have access to resources that will enable you to effectively explore possibilities with your customer?** If so, who and what are they? If not, how can you get them? Will your customer reciprocate with access to their own resources to align with yours? If so, why?

6. **Are you willing to invest your assets to explore possibilities with your customer?** Are you prepared to set an example for your team by investing your own time? Are you prepared to lead your team in these efforts, and initiate and manage internal collaboration before attempting external collaboration with your customer? Exactly how will you accomplish this?

Vision the Success: Visualizing Future Potential Value with Your Customer

YOUR DILIGENT RESEARCH has equipped you with an understanding of what your customer cares most about and, based on the knowledge and credibility you've established, they've engaged with you in an exploration of possibilities before there's a specific opportunity to discuss. Without the pressure of an RFP deadline or multiple rivals competing for the same piece of business, your interactions with your customer are more relaxed and comfortable. They're not looking to buy; you're not trying to sell. And rather than having a predictable conversation about how your solutions will indisputably fulfill the customer's needs, you can focus the dialogue on what you already know they care about. You can help them build a vision of their own success and begin to visualize the future potential value that your organizations can create and co-create together.

A Vision of Customer Success and of Future Potential Value

To build a vision of success with your customer is to provide them with something of great value, especially if this vision enables them to focus more clearly on images of future potential value they haven't previously envisioned. The concept of *vision* can be defined in two forms: as a verb, *vision* means picturing something mentally; as a noun, its meaning becomes perceiving or imagining something that may not be real. Both contexts matter in your quest to move with your customer into the next level of engagement, because most people can't converse credibly about something that they haven't at least contemplated or envisioned. By helping your customer vision what their future success might look like, and then helping them see how to make that real, you distinguish yourself from the crowd of vendors and suppliers that only show up when it's time to sell something. And this vision of making that future success real will include you and your organization, if you ultimately have value to add.

Customers consider themselves successful when a positive outcome they have envisioned as possible is achieved and becomes a reality. Your aspiration is to help them create that vision, but you can't expect to simply walk into a customer's office and start visioning. It just doesn't happen that way.

If, on the other hand, through your research you've come to understand what your customer cares most about and, through your exploration with them you've identified areas of potential interest, then you've probably accrued enough credibility to facilitate a discussion about their future success at meeting and exceeding objectives, as well as how you might add value to their efforts. Based on the work that you've completed through your execution of Strategies 1 and 2, you can identify specific areas of focus and suggest a collaborative discussion around these areas with confidence because you know their priorities. All you're asking your customer to do is talk with you about the things that you've already validated they care about.

Most customers relate best to visioning exercises when the success they visualize is focused on one of the following areas:

- **Accelerating growth.** All companies expect some level of expansion within their businesses, but if you can enable growth to happen more quickly than it would have otherwise, then you can potentially provide value to your customer. Think of it this way: if your offerings will not somehow enable growth for your customer (or at least mitigate decline), then why would they buy from you?

And do you really want to sell your customer something they don't need or want?

- **Reducing costs.** When top-line growth is challenging for your customer, or insufficient to generate the anticipated profit margins, you and your organization may have solutions, products, resources, expertise, best practices, or services that can help. Since the recession that began in 2008, customers have become significantly more willing to accept a trusted supplier's ideas as to how they might improve their businesses operationally. When you help your customer operate more efficiently, you potentially add value to their business.

- **Driving innovation.** Innovation can be a powerful differentiator for an organization, but wanting to innovate and actually doing so can be two very different things. Consequently, some organizations look for ways to go to market with new ideas and offerings that are the result of co-innovation with key suppliers and partners. Helping your customer drive innovation within their business is certainly an example of potential value co-creation, and can make for a most interesting visioning exercise.

- **Gaining competitive advantage.** If the result of your visioning exercise with your customer is the potential for them to gain competitive advantage, then it's a virtual certainty that someone in their organization will be interested in further discussing it with you. The good news is that you will have envisioned potential future value that the customer will want to pursue with you, but be prepared for the inevitable question: "If you do this with us, can you guarantee that you won't do it with our competitors?" It's not an easy question to answer, but in the end, it's a good question to be asked.

- **Creating value for your customer's customers.** Most salespeople and account managers think of their customers primarily as buyers, but be assured that customers are sellers, too. Many similar

strategies and activities that you execute as you engage your customers in pursuit of business are being carried out somewhere
within their organizations, in most cases by people who are not
necessarily your buyers. So try to think beyond your own sales
process and imagine theirs: how will the solutions, products, resources, expertise, best practices, or services that you provide to
your customer ultimately result in added value for your customer's
customers? Potential future value that can be passed on to your
customer's customers can make for a highly compelling visioning
exercise.

- **Growing a loyal customer base.** Most organizations make an
  earnest attempt to gauge their customers' satisfaction, and are to
  be applauded for doing so. But in today's business environment,
  in which speed, customer demands, competition, and stress are
  all steadily mounting, the value of surveys that assess customer
  satisfaction is limited. What really matters today is customer loyalty. If you can suggest future potential value that will enable your
  customer to delight their customers, retain and grow their existing customer relationships, and increase their customers' loyalty,
  there's probably a high-energy visioning exercise in your future.

If only one of these focus areas materializes, you'll still find yourself in
a good place with your customer. And when you do, you'll have a foundation for brainstorming and visualizing the future potential value that your
organizations can create and co-create together. But as you arrive at this
most interesting destination, keep this in mind: when you're visioning success with your customer, authenticity counts. Customers can discern the
difference between a salesperson who just wants to sell them something
and one who genuinely wants them to be successful. You're at this point
(Strategy 3) because you understand and can talk about what's important
to your customer. Through your research and exploration, you've earned
the right to participate in discussions regarding where the customer wants
to go and why. Because you've demonstrated your intent to put the customer first and to focus on what's most important to them, they're much

more likely to vision with you *what* their future success might look like, as well as *how* you might help to make that vision a reality. Rest assured that this is a leap of faith that they certainly wouldn't take if they believed that all you want to do is lure them into a sales conversation. Why would they have their antenna up for this type of sales tactic? Because they've almost certainly "been to that movie" before.

How Today's Customers Define Supplier Value

You can talk about your customer's picture of future success by focusing on such areas as accelerating growth, reducing costs, driving innovation, gaining competitive advantage, creating customer value, and growing a loyal customer base. But it's the customer's belief in your ability to enable their visions to become realities, and to deliver actual value, that will ultimately determine whether they include you and your organization in that vision.

There's no doubt your customer will appreciate your help in coming up with some good ideas, but if you want more than a vigorous handshake and a "thank you," you'll have to show them how working with you will enable—and perhaps accelerate—their future success. The transition from exploring possibilities to visioning success becomes natural when your customer knows that your interest in their success is genuine, and that they'll get there more quickly and assuredly by working with you.

The customer is willing to talk with you because you're the one (and perhaps the only one) who seems interested in discussing the things they care most about—even when they aren't in buying mode. By exploring possibilities, you and your customer are likely to identify at least a few possible value targets—some that might be imminent and others that may be in the distant or not-so-distant future. Now you need to learn where your customer wants to go and why they want to go there.

Practically speaking, you may find that you have to qualify and prioritize your customer's visions of future potential value, because there may be more to consider than you have the resources to cover. There's also the matter of timing: it's important to understand your customer's timeline for realizing this potential value. But the real lynchpin in visioning success with your customer is how you will help them move their visions from an indefinite future into the more specific present.

In existing relationships, you can approach your customers on a regular basis and say, "I'd like to better understand what's going to be important to you over the next 6, 12, or 24 months, so I can plan to allocate my time and resources accordingly." Depending on the nature of the relationship, some suppliers do this more frequently and others less, but most find that their customers are delighted when someone who has created and co-created value with them in the past checks in to see how and where things are going.

These discussions with your customer provide an ideal environment for listening and picking up on any clues or hints they may reveal about their priorities, objectives, aspirations, and motivations. Sometimes, you'll find multiple areas of potential value creation, so keep in mind that you need to understand more than just how your customer prioritizes these potential value targets; at some point, you'll need to determine how your own organization will prioritize them on behalf of the customer.

Before you get to that conversation, you should be prepared to answer the question, "Why *you*?" It's not inevitable that your customer will ask, but don't be caught without an answer if they do. Remember, it's all about how you can help them get to where they want to go, so you should be able to respond transparently and unequivocally: "It's because my organization and I can enable you to reach your destination . . . and here's how." Before you face the "Why you?" question, consider carefully whether or not you and your organization actually have what it takes to enable your customer's visions to become realities.

The assets required to explore possibilities with your customer are also required when you're visualizing future potential value with them. Do you have the time to invest in pursuit of this vision? Can you engage the appropriate team members from within your organization accordingly? Are you able to locate and deliver the collective talent required to vision success with that customer? And, even if you are able to bring the knowledge, skills, and expertise to get started, do you have access to the tools and technology that will enable your engagement with your customer to be effective? If you can't answer these questions in the affirmative, you probably need to wait until you can do so before proceeding. Be realistic about your readiness: successful visioning sessions can boost your credibility significantly in the eyes of your customer. But if they feel you can't live up to your promises or make good on your intentions to deliver the value that you envisioned with them, your credibility will likely take a hit.

Understanding Your Customer's Expectations of You

If you want to build a vision of success with your customer, a good place to start is by understanding how they define and measure the value that their suppliers create for them and co-create with them. Figure 3-1 represents a tool that Steve's firm, Performance Methods, Inc. (PMI), developed with the assistance of the Strategic Account Management Association (SAMA), a nonprofit association that helps member companies establish strategic, key, and global account management. Created through the insights of industry leaders from across the globe, as well as their customers, this figure reflects the sixteen most frequently cited value categories regarding how customers define supplier value. When you can identify the characteristics that are important to your customer, you're on your way to focusing your engagement on what they value most in their interactions with their suppliers.

You've made yourself a student of your customer and you've explored possibilities together. Transitioning from simply exploring possibilities into visioning success, you'll need to spend a little more time thinking like your customer.

Until you actually discuss value expectations with your customer, you won't be certain which of these categories will matter most to them. But you should have enough information and early insight to develop a short list based on what you've learned through your research and exploration. As you review these sixteen statements, think about which four your customer might put at the top of their priority list, and whether your organization can fulfill these needs.

WOULD YOUR CUSTOMER AGREE WITH THESE STATEMENTS?

	YES*	NO
1. You make it easy for us to do business with you		
2. You resolve our problems and conflicts as they arise		
3. You understand our business and our industry		
4. You listen to our needs before talking about your offerings		
5. You consult with us with an intent to solve our business problems		
6. You dedicate the resources that will enable us to work effectively together		
7. You provide us with preferred pricing and contract terms		
8. You align your team members with ours		
9. You approach our business strategically and not just transactionally when we're buying		
10. You plan the future together with us even when we are not buying		
11. You develop relationships between our executives and yours		
12. You help us understand the specific value of your offerings		
13. You help us assess your performance with mutually acceptable metrics		
14. You share best practices and industry knowledge that will add value to our business		
15. You provide a single point of contact to us for strategy and decision-making		
16. You provide an internal advocate for us that will be focused on our specific needs		

* What evidence do you have that your "yes" answers are true?

Figure 3-1. How customers define supplier value.

1. **"You make it easy for us to do business with you."** This may seem like table stakes in today's business environment, but some suppliers are just more challenging to do business with than others. Add this one to your list if your customer wants you to be easy to engage with, especially if you or another supplier in your space hasn't been easy to work with in the past. *How easy is it for your customers to do business with you and your organization?*

2. **"You resolve our problems and conflicts as they arise."** Put simply, this means when it breaks, you fix it, and you fix it promptly. Most people in B2B relationships understand that something is bound to go wrong somewhere along the way. But even when it's expected, customers pressured by the speed of business feel a need to know that you will make every possible effort to resolve issues quickly. *Do you minimize your customers' stress by resolving problems right away, or do they sometimes feel they have to keep after you to get things done?*

3. **"You understand our business and our industry."** This is not so challenging when all of your business happens in one industry—such as finance or information technology—but what if your accounts span several or even many industries? *Do you know as much as you should about your customer's business and industry?*

4. **"You listen to our needs before talking about your offerings."** We've all been there: the meeting begins and the salesperson or account manager launches into "product-speak," "company-speak," or "me-speak" and proceeds to talk about things that the buyer doesn't care about. Why does this happen all of the time all over the world? Because under stress and pressure, salespeople tend to revert to their comfort zones and talk too much about things they are comfortable talking about. *Do you ever find yourself talking too much about you and yours before listening carefully to what's on your customer's mind?*

5. **"You consult with us with an intent to solve our business problems."** This may sound the same as statement 2, but there's a difference, and it's more than subtle. This statement is not about fixing something that's broken; it's about providing expertise and best practices that could prevent the breakage from happening at all. (Note that we say "consult with," not "sell to.") Your customer is unlikely to consult with people they don't trust

and through your execution of Strategies 1 and 2, you've ideally demonstrated trustworthy behaviors. *Do you engage consultatively with your customers, and do they see you as a business problem solver?*

6. **"You dedicate the resources that will enable us to work effectively together."** If dedicated resources are important to your customer, this can be huge. When you charge specific people with becoming knowledgeable about your customer's business and their history with your organization, the benefits to your customer can be significant. Most selling and account management organizations will commit resources to a customer, but that doesn't necessarily mean that the two parties work well together. *Does your organization dedicate resources to support your customers, and if so, do your resources engage efficiently and effectively?*

7. **"You provide us with preferred pricing and contract terms."** Some customers only seem to care about price, or at least that's how it feels when you talk with their procurement staff. But in almost every case, there are others within your customer's organization who believe that their relationship with you is about more than just price and your contract terms. In commodity-like buying/selling environments, this is likely to be a significant factor, but even then, you'll almost always find that your customer has other value expectations. *Did you ever believe that a customer based a decision solely on price, only to find out later that other factors also influenced their decision?*

8. **"You align your team members with ours."** The result of too many people from your team trying to interact with too many people from your customer's team can be a customer that thinks doing business with you is complicated and convoluted. Do you make it clear who from your team should be talking with whom from theirs in the normal course of doing business together? *Is*

it ever difficult for customers to navigate your organization and connect with the right people to get things done, and if so, can you simplify this for them?

9. **"You approach our business strategically, not just transactionally when we're buying."** Most customers want to know that you care enough about your relationship with them to invest time even when they're not buying. Customers that feel this way tend to care about their relationship with you, and it's likely they engage with their own customers in much the same way. In cases where the customer has done substantial business with you in the past, and has the potential to do so again in the future, it's hard to justify not making time for them simply because you're not pursuing an active opportunity. *Do your customers know that you're there for them, even when there's no opportunity at hand?*

10. **"You plan the future together with us, even when we're not buying."** In a new customer relationship, you may not yet have earned the right to plan together with your customer. But when you and your customer have a history of value creation and co-creation, it's hard to imagine that either party would not be interested in opportunities to align with the other's plans for the ultimate purpose of further mutual value creation. Your customer has to plan ahead and so do you, whether it's at the sales territory level, sales opportunity level, or the account level. When you're planning, seeking input from your customer makes sense and your customer may feel similarly about your having input into their plans. *Do you invest time into planning with your customers, and do you seek their input into your own plans?*

11. **"Your organization develops relationships between your executives and ours."** Executive or peer-to-peer relationships are extremely valuable to some customers, while others don't seem

to care whether there's senior-level involvement or not, as long as your sales or account team is getting the job done. The motives of customers who genuinely value senior-level relationships with peers tend to range from wanting easy access to the ultimate decision makers to simply wanting to connect at peer levels out of a sense of political appropriateness. Whatever the motivation, if your customer likes to do business this way, then you should make time to build, nurture, and manage these relationships, because when they matter, they matter a lot. *If a customer values engagement at the highest organizational levels, do you do your part to facilitate peer-to-peer relationships between your leadership and theirs?*

12. **"You help us understand the specific value of your offerings."** At some point, your customer will have to vouch for the value that you and your organization have created on their behalf. This may be because procurement is challenging your pricing, or another provider is trying to displace you by claiming to deliver more at a lower price. Or your customer may need to validate that they have completed a project or purchase on time and on budget. Whatever the reason, it's always to your advantage if your customer can talk about the value of your offering both internally, within their organization, and externally, with your potential customers. *If your customers were asked to defend why they chose you, how confident are you that they can explain your value?*

13. **"You help us assess your performance with mutually acceptable metrics."** Like never before, customers are being challenged to conduct business on time, on budget, and per plan, so they need ways to measure the success of the business they do with you. This requires metrics, and your best metrics will be those you build together with your customer. If you're willing to subject yourself to accountability, you can empower your cus-

tomer to assess your performance using a measuring stick that you can help develop. They'll likely make this assessment with or without your help, so why wouldn't you want to provide the appropriate input and data from your organization to support their efforts? *Are you willing to work with your customers to build a set of mutual metrics for assessing your performance?*

14. **"You share best practices and industry knowledge that add value to our business."** Sharing best practices and industry knowledge is one of the most underutilized forms of customer-defined value; it's huge for those customers who understand it can help them improve their business. Peter Ostrow, Vice President and Research Group Director, Sales Effectiveness and Customer Management at Aberdeen Group, offers this perspective: "Today's empowered customers force sellers to give up on generic sales pitches, and to find a way to personalize the first, and every, conversation they hold with their buyers. In four words: Give before you get." When you help your customer improve their business, you create value with them in ways that are not easily replicated by your competitors. *Do you share best practices and industry knowledge with your customers when you have the opportunity to do so, even when they're not buying?*

15. **"You provide us with a single point of contact for strategy and decision making."** In today's complex business environment, it's virtually impossible for one person to serve as the only contact for a customer, especially if the buying/selling environment is complex, or if the relationship between the parties is considered strategic in nature. For some customers, it's especially important to know who to call if something is amiss; it reduces their sense of risk when they know they can count on their go-to person when they need a rapid response or access to special resources. *Do customers ever ask you for a single point of*

contact for strategy and decision making, and if so, do you some-times find yourself serving in this role?

16. **"You provide us with an internal advocate who will focus on our specific needs."** Your customer wants to know that in times of need, someone in your organization, maybe at the executive level or someone with access to corporate resources, will advocate for them. This doesn't necessarily indicate a lack confidence in you, and you may in fact be that customer advocate. But in situations where the volume of current and future business is considerable and the pressure for the customer to perform is intense, it can be a great comfort for them to know that some-one within your organization (sometimes in addition to you) can step in as needed on their behalf. *When a customer requires a special level of advocacy within your organization, are you able to carry this load by yourself?*

Now that you've thought about each category as it relates to your cus-tomer, identify the top four areas that you believe are most important to them, and make sure that you're prepared to have a conversation about each one. Later, you'll want to validate what you've selected with your cus-tomer as a way of elevating the conversation to the next level. But for the time being, you're developing and building a collaborative vision of cus-tomer success that, if it's compelling enough, will enable you to elevate your conversation and gain commitment to pursue specific value targets with your customer.

Developing a Collaborative Vision of Customer Success

When you and your customer vision together and visualize a successful future that includes you, your customer learns that you and your organi-zation intend to enable their path to success. At the same time, you're increasing the likelihood that you'll be the one they partner with to help them create this successful future. As you prepare to evolve into Strategy 4 and develop or identify your next opportunity, it's likely that your competitors would envy the kind of relationship with your customer that you now have. We urge you to keep several things in mind as you use the customer-defined value tool featured in Figure 3-1, and apply the following concepts to build and solidify a vision of success with your customer:

- **Every customer defines value differently**. At the organizational level, a company's value expectations tend to be shaped by its culture, guiding principles, and market dynamics, among other factors. Expect to find different visions of value from different people on your customer's team; value expectations tend to be personal in nature, and specific to the business and life experiences of the individual.

- **No customer values all of the categories on the list**. That's a good thing, because it's unlikely that your organization can afford to provide all sixteen for every customer, and do them well. The potential downside of focusing on the wrong areas includes wasted time, lost credibility, annoyed customers, and an unclear vision of what could have been.

- **All customers value some of the categories listed**. The compelling potential upside of collaboratively determining value with your customer includes investing your time properly, growing your credibility, and delighting your customer. Additionally, you'll be able to focus more clearly on the path to potential future value.

Visioning success and visualizing future potential value is about helping your customer determine what future success looks like and how you and your organization can help them get there. In a world that is long on vendors and short on partners, Strategy 3 can be significant if your objective is to be the latter rather than the former. You're well positioned to move forward with your customer because you've done your due diligence and research, and you've explored possibilities together. Add the picture of success that your customer and you have visualized together, and you're on the threshold of creating a new opportunity. Now it's time to elevate the conversation with your customer by defining, prioritizing, and pursuing your value targets.

Testing the Effectiveness of Your Visioning

The following six sets of questions will help you determine the effectiveness of your visioning with your customer:

1. **Based on what you learned from your visioning exercise, is your customer's future success likely to ultimately connect with either revenue growth or cost reduction?** If so, why? If neither, why not? How have your customer's revenues and costs been trending over the past 12 months?

2. **Is your customer's future success likely to result from driving more innovation from within their business?** If so, why? Does your customer have a culture of innovation? Does your customer innovate and co-innovate with their customers?

3. **Will you and your organization be able to help your customer develop and sustain competitive advantage?** When your customer wins business, what are the reasons for it, and why? Are any of your customer's competitors your customers? How is your customer perceived in their market(s)?

4. **Will you and your organization be able to help your customer create or co-create value with their customers?** For example, how can you help your customer increase the loyalty of their customers? Does your customer have a relatively small percentage of customers that constitutes a relatively large percentage of their revenues?

5. **What are your top four categories of customer-defined value?** If you ask your sales/account team members, how will they answer? If you ask your customer's team members, how will they

answer? How much can you reasonably deliver based on the products, resources, expertise, best practices, and services that your customer requires?

6. **Are you able to prioritize your top four categories of customer-defined value?** If you had developed this list 6 months ago, would the priorities have been different? If so, why and how? If you can only deliver on one of your top four over the next 6 months, which would you prioritize first from your customer's perspective? Why?

STRATEGY 4

Elevate the Conversation: Defining and Pursuing Customer Value Targets

LET'S TAKE A LOOK at where we are: as you move from visioning success with your customer into Strategy 4, you are at a critical juncture. You're still before the sale and you've worked hard to get here, but there's more work to do with your customer if you ever want to engage with them in a real opportunity. Your research, exploration, and visioning have led you to the threshold of developing new business, and you're just about to step across.

You have good reason to be confident, and it's because of how you've engaged with your customer up to this point. Through your research, you've learned about their organization, and you're tuned in to the news and developments that are impacting their world. You've learned about their business culture and how they're perceived within their industry. You have a sense of the drivers, objectives, and challenges that are confronting your customer, as well as how they create business value with their customers and partners through the value proposition they bring to their markets. You know who they consider to be their toughest competitors, and you have insight into how they make buying decisions. You've also gathered as much information as you can directly from customer contacts that are accessible to you, as well as through the Internet and social media. Finally, if the customer is an existing one, you know what you need to know about your organization's history with them. You've leveraged all of the resources at your disposal, including customer information that resides within your organization's CRM solution and your colleagues who have experience with your customer.

Your diligence as a student of your customer means you can identify the areas they consider most important, understand how they determine priorities, and discuss topics of greatest impact to their organization. Your ability to explore areas of potential interest has moved you directly into the realm of meaningful dialogue about specifics, whether it includes growing their business, meeting their objectives, delighting their own customers, or gaining advantage over their competitors. You're in a position to know what's most relevant to your customer because together you've explored the possibilities, and together you have begun to build a vision of their success by imagining what could be accomplished through partnering with you and your organization. You've earned the right to a deeper discussion; you've invested the time, effort, and resources, and it's clear that you are authentically interested in helping the customer succeed.

At this point, your customer may even have granted you some opportunities for early collaboration around what a partnership with your organization might look like. After all, you've helped them paint the picture of their own success and how they can make it real within their organization. Whether their vision of success focuses on accelerating growth, reducing costs, driving innovation, gaining competitive advantage, creating value, or increasing loyalty, you and your customer have collaborated to brainstorm what's within the realm of the possible. Your credibility has grown, and it's a direct result of how you have engaged. The customer sees you as genuine, authentic, and indisputably different from the other suppliers that they work with, or who want to work with them.

Your investment has brought you to the next level of engagement. You are ready to help your customer define the targets for value creation that you will pursue together. You're poised to make the important transition from *before* to *during* the sale. But in order to make the leap from pre-opportunity into the opportunity phase, you'll have to *elevate the conver-*

sation with your customer, which means that you will ascend to a level of communication that is less crowded, less noisy, and significantly less bumpy than the level at which most of your competitors now find themselves.

A Word of Caution About Your Customer Conversations

Customer conversations do not elevate haphazardly, without reason. You're able to extend and expand your dialogue with the customer because they see significant upside potential for themselves and their business. Pushing, pressuring, or otherwise attempting to manipulate your customer doesn't work, especially if your goal is to establish a collaborative, ongoing relationship that creates value for both organizations.

Think of it this way: it is as difficult to trust a person who is controlling, overbearing, and manipulative as it is not to trust someone who does his or her homework, explores possibilities, helps create a vision of success, and elevates the conversation because he or she can engage differently. You most definitely want to be the latter. When you engage in a dialogue that reflects the homework you've done and your genuine understanding of what's important to your customer, they will almost certainly feel more aligned with you. In contrast, your competitors who didn't bother to invest the time or effort will likely experience the reverse. This is when you see the gap widen between you and the competition. You've raised the bar, and you can bet that your customer has noticed.

Salespeople and account managers who go beyond the sales process tell us their customers note a big difference in how they engage. When you follow the twelve *Engage/Win/Grow* strategies, you become a significant component of your organization's value proposition. You become a part of that difference.

Remember, a customer conversation is one that focuses on the customer, and should never be confused with a conversation about a product or business unit that you represent. Resist the temptation to launch into a discussion of your favorite offering, even when you feel confident that you can predict how it will play out with your customer. Now is simply not the time, and it's a virtual certainty that you won't get the results you're seeking in the end.

Containing your enthusiasm requires discipline, and it's counterintuitive for some salespeople. But breaking into "sales-speak" is the worst thing you can do at this moment, because there's still no opportunity yet. If you go into sales mode now, you'll undo much of what you've accomplished with Strategies 1 through 3, and all that effort will have been for naught.

Bob Kelly, Chairman of the Sales Management Association, offers this perspective:

"Great sales organizations and the best salespeople are masterful in applying frameworks, not in slavishly following routine. The former takes judgment, adaptation, an openness to inquiry, and skilled experience. Sales organizations make mistakes when, in the interest of productivity, they take away salespeople's discretion or over-rely on process at the expense of innovation. Our research shows that emphasizing the enforcement of prescriptive activity models and processes has a negative effect on firm performance, while sales organizations with greater decision-making autonomy are more likely to excel."

When you engage in a way that is focused on your value to the customer, rather than their value to you, the customer will be willing, and perhaps even eager, to advance their dialogue with you and collaborate to develop customer value targets.

Focusing on the Customer Value Target

A *customer value target* has three components that combine the essential considerations for effectively targeting customer value:

1. *What* your customer needs to do to meet and exceed a specific objective.

2. *How* you and your organization will help your customer meet this objective.

3. *Why* this matters to both parties: your customer first, and then you.

When you think about a customer value target, the emphasis should be on the customer. It's about their target, not yours. What must they do to advance their business objectives? You should also be thinking about how you will help them. Are you actually able to assist with their pursuit of a specific area of potential value? Finally, you should be asking yourself why it matters—first to your customer, and then to you. Is the potential value target compelling and high-impact enough to result in your customer taking action? And is it compelling enough for you and your own organization to take action?

The customer value target concept is simple yet powerful, and when you get it right, the impact can be dramatic. As we prepare for a deeper dive into customer value targets and how they can help you elevate your customer conversations, and ultimately develop new sales opportunities, keep these ideas in mind:

- **The customer value target is not about the value that you and your organization hope to gain from future business with your customer.** It's not a commission check or a deal that you are pushing to close. It's the *customer's* value target, supported and re-sourced by you and the products, resources, expertise, and services that you will bring to equip and enable them to be successful. Your ability to do this is directly connected to the diligence of your re-search, exploration, and visioning.

- **The customer value target is about the potential value that can be created or co-created by working collaboratively with your customer.** This potential value is defined in terms of what's important to your customer, and thanks again to your research, exploration, and visioning, you don't have to guess what that is.

Further, because your focus is squarely on what matters most to your customer, your level of engagement is far beyond that of a typical vendor and more like that of a partner.

- **There is nothing random about a customer value target because it is highly focused and targeted to what you now know about how your customer defines value.** You're at this level of engagement because you've engaged effectively with your customer. Rather than pushing your "special of the month" or pressuring your customer to consider an alternative (and possibly nonessential) product line that your organization offers, you have done your homework, given the customer a reason to engage, and helped them build a picture of how they can achieve success.

So you have arrived at the opportunity crossroads, and most routes favor you. This is where you can potentially earn the exclusive right to conduct an evaluation, or shape the requirements of an RFP that will soon be issued. But unless you are able to develop a compelling customer value target and elevate the conversation with your customer accordingly, you'll find yourself staying right where you are: *before the sale.*

Elevating the Conversation

Whether they're personal in nature or professional and business oriented, conversations need a reason to elevate. In our customer-driven world, your customer simply doesn't have time for topics that aren't important to their success, and you don't either. On the other hand, when you do your homework, approach your customer with a willingness and readiness to focus on what matters most to them, and demonstrate an authentic desire to help them be successful (even without a sale in sight), your customer is likely to notice. This is why we call it a customer value target, not a supplier value target, or even just a value target.

To elevate your customer conversation to a new level, you must be able to demonstrate that you clearly understand what they want to do, how you can help them, and why it matters to them. The question is, how do you do that? The good news is that, through Strategies 1 to 3, you've already accomplished much of what you need to get started. Let's look at what it takes to develop a compelling customer value target with your customer.

What Your Customer Needs to Do. Demonstrating that you understand what's happening in your customer's world can lead quite naturally into a conversation about how you might be able to help. You can launch that discussion by validating what you learned from your research and through your exploration with your customer (see Figure 2-1). Then give your customer the opportunity to confirm your understanding, or clarify what you didn't get right; let them tell you what they need to do.

Which of these statements, coming from your customer, would seem most likely to ring true? As you read each one, think about how you can help them meet that objective.

- **"We need to grow and develop our organization."** If your customer's business is expanding through acquisition or rapid organic growth, they may need assistance dealing with the changes confronting them as a result. *If your own company has assisted another customer with organizational development challenges, what lessons learned and best practices might be helpful to this customer?*

- **"Our world has changed and there's no going back, so we need to adapt to our new business environment."** Many businesses felt this way after the 2008 recession, and some are still adapting their businesses to this new reality. *Are there ways you can help your customer with their transition? Has your organization had a similar experience?*

- **"As an organization, we need to evolve from an emphasis on our products to a greater focus on our customers."** Have you ever known a company that developed a successful business through product excellence, only to find out one day that their products weren't so unique, and their customers not so loyal? *If your organization has helped other customers that were evolving their business cultures, can you provide similar value to this customer?*

- **"We want to be perceived differently within our industry, so we need to change the way we do business."** Most industries have acknowledged leaders, and we're pleased to highlight a number of them in the case studies we've included in this book. But industry leadership comes with a price: the investment in people, processes, technology, and infrastructure can be significant. *If you're doing business with other industry leaders, how have you helped them ascend to and sustain their leadership position?*

- **"External drivers and market pressures are forcing our organization to take action."** We fully unpack the importance of drivers, objectives, and challenges in Section II, but for now, consider the difficulties that businesses face when they are confronted by external forces outside their control. *Do you understand what your customer is doing to meet objectives, and can you help them overcome the challenges facing their business?*

- **"We need to strengthen our value proposition for each market we serve."** Your customer may need to broaden their portfolio, improve quality, or reduce their prices/costs, and they may need to partner with a supplier to make this happen. *Do you understand your customer's value proposition for each of their primary markets? If so, how can you and your organization add value?*

- **"Our customers expect more from us than ever before, so we need to get more value from the suppliers we do business with."** This is great news, because your customer wants you to be more than a supplier or a vendor—they're asking you to partner with them. The bad news is that others may be hearing it, too! *How can you and your organization create value for your customer's customers?*

- **"Our network of partners is vital to the health of our business, and we need to create more value for the organizations that compose that network."** If your customer goes to market through a network of distributors, agents, brokers, or resellers, then any value you add to these sell-through relationships can be significant, especially when those partners are not exclusive to your customer. *If you have experience with other customers that had comparable go-to-market strategies, how were you able to create value that could be passed on to their partners?*

- **"We have been losing market share to a major rival, and we need to find ways to be more competitive against this organization."** Practically every company has a top competitor (or two or three), and these competitive wins and losses have been engrained into your customer's culture and folklore. *If you've created value that has enabled another organization to gain competitive advantage in their markets, can the lessons learned be shared with your customer?*

- **"For greater efficiency, we need to engage suppliers that adapt how they do business to our buying processes."** Over the years, buyers and sellers have struggled to find ways to do business together more effectively, and the recent rise of procurement isn't likely to subside as global economies continue to recover from the recession. Most organizations have taken a hard look at how they procure the things they need, and some even outsource this function in search of greater efficiencies. Like it or not, you can expect the percentage of sales that go to RFPs in the future to increase. *What can you do to align more seamlessly with how your customer wants to do business?*

- **"We are planning a major investment in training and developing our people, and we need to find ways to do it as efficiently and effectively as possible."** We weren't kidding about those CEOs we mentioned in the Introduction: they have no greater business asset than their people, not even their customers. Organizations are very sensitive about investing in their people, and decisions to do so are usually preceded by great thought and discussion. *If your organization has undertaken this type of initiative (or you have a* *customer that has), are there ways you can add value to your customer's decision to invest in their people?*

- **"Based on our volumes, we believe we should be receiving more value from your organization than we're getting right now."** This is a customer comment that most salespeople and account managers dread hearing. But if your customer feels this way, then you certainly need to know, because that perception won't go away unless you take action. *Are there ways you can enable your customer to get more value from the money that they currently spend with you?*

Remember, to elevate the conversation with your customer, you only have to develop one area of need, and you're on your way to defining your customer value target. In order to focus on what your customer needs to do, introspection and discussion within your own organization are a must. Can you help your customer pursue this future potential value, and if so, how?

How You Will Help Your Customer Do It. If you're going to be successful in elevating the conversation with your customer, your next step is determining, and articulating, how you (and the resources available to you) will help your customer address their needs and achieve the success that they have envisioned with you. In other words, as a supplier that is beginning to demonstrate an authentic willingness to partner with your customer, what types of value can you provide to increase their likelihood of success?

When you visioned future potential value with your customer in Strategy 3, you developed a shortlist of customer-defined supplier value categories (based on Figure 3-1) by thinking like your customer. Now, it's time to validate your selections, and the only way to do it is directly with your customer. You and your customer need to collaborate and discuss the shortlist of items you've developed so you can confirm that you are on the right track in terms of how you can best help them. And don't forget to validate their commitment to move forward with you; you've made quite an investment, and it's not too much to ask your customer for a little assurance as you prepare to move forward together.

This is a pivotal point in your transition from pre-opportunity into the pursuit of a newly minted sales opportunity, and your evolution from *before the sale* to *during the sale*. For each item on your value short list, prepare to participate in an elevated customer conversation when you engage as follows:

1. **"We'll make it easier for you to do business with us."** If this is one of your selections, it's probably because your customer feels that you haven't been easy in the past, or their current supplier isn't. Be prepared for them to ask what's going to be different this time around.

2. **"When problems occur and issues arise, we will handle them quickly and deliberately."** The speed of business today doesn't allow most companies to wait for problem resolution. If this item made your list, be aware that your customer's sense of business risk rises the longer they have to wait for your organization's response to their issues.

3. **"We'll make it our business to learn more about your business."** Depending on the area of need that you and your customer are going to pursue, it may be necessary for you and your team members to become even more insightful about your customer's business. This will require a time investment on your end. You might ask your customer to agree to help you further your understanding, and even allow you and your organization to participate in some of their internal training, learning, and development resources in the spirit of partnership.

4. **"We're going to continue our focus on listening to you."** If this is one of your selections, chances are good that your customer has already benefited from your willingness to listen, as well as from the patience and discipline you demonstrated in doing so. Consider coaching your team members that it's important to

refrain from bombarding customers with too much discussion of solutions or products when listening is the key objective.

5. **"We'll consult with you and help you solve your business problems."** If this selection will contribute to how you help your customer pursue their value targets, then you're in an especially favorable position. Customers typically aren't interested in consulting with suppliers that they don't consider trustworthy, and they only consult with those that they believe have something to offer.

6. **"We'll commit the resources and expertise required to help you meet your objective."** The cost of doing business should certainly be considered here, and there are plenty of examples of a supplier's resources and expertise making a significant impact on a customer relationship. One word of caution: be sure to have your internal house in order before running the risk of over-commitment and under-delivery with your customer.

7. **"We will provide special pricing and terms to help you through a difficult situation."** While many first-draft shortlists include this item, few finished versions retain it after the customer validation process. No matter how your customer defines value, it is clear that early discounting occurs far too frequently. If special pricing matters to your customer, try to ensure that you won't get stuck at artificially low price points later because you tried to do the right thing today.

8. **"We're going to ensure that your people know who to connect with on our team, and how to best engage with them."** One consistent complaint from customers is the difficulties they experience in navigating their supplier organizations, and having to endure "slow no's" (the feeling a customer gets when it takes too long to get an answer from their supplier) to their requests. If team-to-team alignment is important to your customer, then

the speed of doing business probably is as well. Consider letting your customer know in advance when there may be a longer wait than anticipated.

9. **"We're strategically committed to our relationship with you, even when you're not buying."** It's hard to be strategic and transactional with your customer at the same time. They know this, and they also understand that you have your own objectives to meet. But the subtlety here is manifested in your willingness to be there for the customer when they aren't buying. They probably assume this will be true if they're pursuing value targets with you, but why not be sure? Developing an ongoing dialogue with your customer and offering opinions and observations about their business, market, and competitors sends a strong message that you are committed to their success.

10. **"We're prepared to engage in planning activities so that we can chart a successful future together."** Something special happens when a customer and supplier meet at the planning table together. If this item appeals to your customer, then it should come as no surprise that they have explored, visioned, and are about to elevate their conversation with you. We'll discuss more about planning in Sections II and III, but for now, be advised that these types of activities typically only occur when the customer sees you as being strategic to their business.

11. **"We're interested in developing more peer-to-peer relationships between our senior leaders and yours."** If this is important to your customer, then you've got to make it a priority, and there can be a huge upside. But be cautioned that it's rarely a good idea to bring your executives into customer meetings without some coaching first; even with the best intentions, executives who don't understand as much as you do about your customer, their world, and your history together can inadvertently

do more harm than good. If you don't prepare them properly, you could be putting yourself at unnecessary risk.

12. **"We will invest the time to ensure that you understand the value that we propose to deliver."** Customers have to justify their expenditures more than ever before, and visits to procurement sometimes mean they have to explain why they are doing so much business with your organization. Your customer may need some assistance in reporting the successful outcome of a project that they've completed with you, so it can be helpful to both parties if they understand and can describe the value that you bring (and have brought) to them. A course in accounting and financial fundamentals for non-finance people can provide a foundation for having that conversation.

13. **"We're prepared to have our performance measured, and will help you develop the metrics to evaluate our success."** In today's business environment, risk mitigation is a growing consideration, and when you proactively suggest measurement and accountability, it sends a powerful message to your customer. If performance measurement is especially critical, consider asking your customer to participate in defining metrics, and ensure that at least some measures look at performance on both sides: yours and your customer's.

14. **"By pursuing this type of value target with other customers, we've gained knowledge, and we'd like to share some of our learnings and best practices with you."** If your customer values the knowledge and expertise that you and your team can bring, then this can be huge. Sharing what you know about what has worked for others (particularly those within your customer's industry) can have a profound impact on your relationship. If you can bring best practices to better enable your customer's pursuit of their value targets, then your credibility is likely to rise.

15. **"We're willing to establish a central focal point within our organization to make your strategy and decision making easier and faster."** In time-critical projects, the ability to get questions answered and requests addressed quickly is imperative, yet many customers tell us that they consider their suppliers' painfully slow decision processes to be problematic. If this is a factor for your customer, then you need to mitigate their potentially difficult navigation and long wait times when working with your organization (which sometimes means you're the one who has to step up).

16. **"We have identified a sponsor from within our organization that will advocate on your behalf."** Depending on the amount of business that you do with the customer (or the magnitude of the value target that you'll pursue together), providing your customer with a sponsor can add a meaningful dimension to your relationship. Having an internal advocate can make a significant difference when it comes to getting things done, so why not ask your customer to reciprocate with a sponsor/advocate for your organization on their side?

Focused on what your customer needs to do and equipped with your selections of how you will help them do it, you're almost ready to finalize your customer value target and move forward with a fully qualified opportunity. But one thing remains before you can feel fully confident that you've elevated your conversation and are ready to put *Before the Sale* behind you. Is the upside of taking action compelling enough for your customer and you to commit to going the distance during the sale? In other words, this customer value target becomes a qualified sales opportunity if, and only if, it matters enough to both parties to see it through.

Why This Matters to Your Customer (and to You). Less a function of data and more a function of insight, the question has now become whether to proceed or not. You should be feeling confident at this point, because what you've researched, explored, and visioned with your customer is about to become elevated into a sales opportunity. You've closed the gap from what was imagined to what is much more real, and in the process, you've collaborated with your customer about the things that matter most to them.

You're almost there, but you don't want to endure a false start in pursuit of a value target that wasn't qualified. If the success that you visioned so effectively with your customer in Strategy 3 is about to become a reality, it is because both parties have reason to believe that the potential upside to moving forward together far outweighs the downside to doing nothing. So it's time to make the call: will you move forward into *During the Sale* and pursue your new opportunity? If you believe in your execution of Strategies 1 to 4, and the effectiveness of your customer engagement, why wouldn't you?

Defining Your Customer Value Targets

Figure 4-1 provides a hypothetical example of how to move from visioning possibilities with your customer into an elevated conversation, by answering these questions: (1) What does your customer need to do? (2) How will you help them do it? (3) Why does it matter?

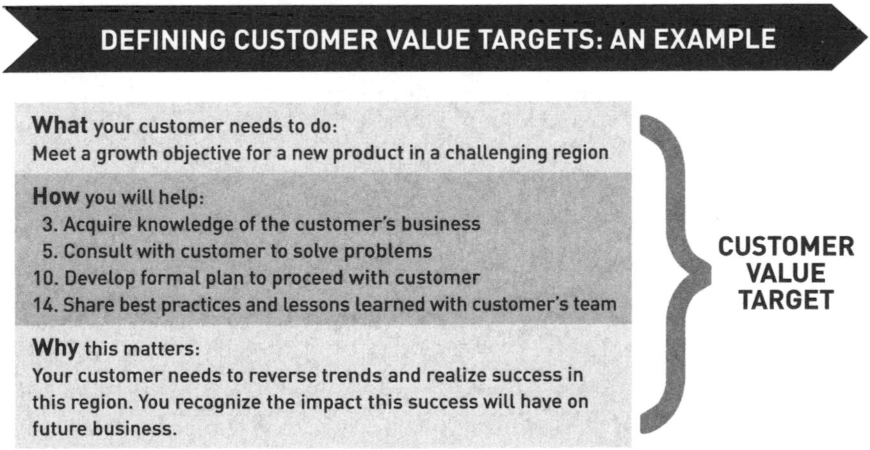

DEFINING CUSTOMER VALUE TARGETS: AN EXAMPLE

What your customer needs to do:
Meet a growth objective for a new product in a challenging region

How you will help:
3. Acquire knowledge of the customer's business
5. Consult with customer to solve problems
10. Develop formal plan to proceed with customer
14. Share best practices and lessons learned with customer's team

Why this matters:
Your customer needs to reverse trends and realize success in this region. You recognize the impact this success will have on future business.

CUSTOMER VALUE TARGET

Figure 4-1. Defining customer value targets: an example.

While you and your customer are exploring possibilities together, they reveal that they're under pressure to meet a growth objective for a planned new product launch in a specific region. Based on your research, you know this region and market have been difficult for your customer in the past, and they're likely to face many of the same challenges this time around. Through visioning discussions, you and your customer have agreed on the future potential value of a successful product launch within this region. After validating your understanding of their value targets from the list of sixteen possibilities we discussed earlier, you determine that, in order to help them, you'll need to do the following:

- Acquire more in-depth knowledge of the customer's business (item 3).

- Engage consultatively with the customer throughout the product launch (item 5).

- Develop a formal plan to proceed with resources and milestones identified (item 10).

- Share best practices and lessons learned with the customer through your organization's experience with other customers doing business in this region (item 14).

Further collaboration with your customer reveals that that the stakes are high because they can't endure another setback in this region. Through internal discussions within your own organization, you determine that success in this project will translate into additional downstream business, and that your investment in items 3, 5, 10, and 14 is appropriate.

When you can articulate a clear understanding of your customer's value target and how you can help them achieve their objective, and receive confirmation that it matters enough for both parties to take action, you've crossed that new business threshold that we alluded to earlier: your pre-opportunity efforts have just moved you into an active sales opportunity.

Evolving from *Before* to *During* the Sale

You've elevated your conversation with your customer through your research, exploration, and visioning together, and you've done so in a way that they feel compelled to take action with you. As you evolve from *before* to *during* the sale, you are more valuable to your customer because you delivered value before there was any promise of an opportunity or commitment to a potential sale. Your credibility is high and your customer treats you differently because you have engaged differently with them. Now, when you meet with your customer, there's even some trust in the room. Make no mistake: you've gained competitive advantage before the actual competition for your new opportunity has begun. Even better, your competitors don't and won't realize it until it's likely too late for them to react properly (and the operative term is *react*).

Did you ever wonder what happened before your customer issued the last RFP you responded to? If you don't know, then there's a good possibility that someone else did the research, exploration, and visioning with your customer, and then elevated the conversation as we've discussed here in Strategy 4. If that someone wasn't you, it should be clear just how far behind you were in pursuing the business behind an RFP that was blind to you but clearly visible to your competitor.

We're sure this will never happen to you again. Next time, as you move from *before* to *during* the sale, you'll leverage the effectiveness of your research, exploration, visioning, and elevation of your customer conversation. You're no longer just another vendor on a bidder's list, because you've engaged differently. You're now in an active opportunity, and you've arrived with significantly more insight than any of your competitors, most of whom haven't been doing their homework, or perhaps weren't even paying attention at all.

Testing the Effectiveness of Your Elevation

The following six sets of questions will help you determine the effectiveness of elevating the conversation with your customer:

1. **Is it clear that your customer value target is focused on your customer's objectives and not yours?** Is it based on one or more of the possibilities that you explored and prioritized with your customer? Does it connect with the vision of success that you developed with them?

2. **How would you describe the level of collaboration in which you and your customer have engaged during the development of your customer value target?** How does it compare with your collaborative discussions with them in the past? How were you able to elevate your conversation while collaborating with them this time?

3. **When you developed the first component of your customer value target (what your customer needs to do), how did you leverage the possibilities that you explored with your customer in Strategy 2?** As your customer conversation elevated, did their priorities change? Did you find yourself exploring new possibilities with them?

4. **When you developed the second component of your customer value target (how you will help your customer do it), how did you leverage the future potential value that you visioned with your customer in Strategy 3?** As your conversation elevated, did the vision of success that you developed with the customer change? If so, how? Did your top four categories of customer-defined value change? If so, how?

5. **When you developed the third component of your customer value target (why it matters to your customer and you), how did you validate the importance of this value target with your customer?** Does your customer feel that that this value target is compelling enough to warrant action and a commitment to move forward with you? Is this value target compelling enough to warrant action and a commitment to move forward with the customer?

6. **When you reflect on the development of your customer value target, how did your research, exploration, and visioning impact your result?** In addition to a strong, mutually agreed upon customer value target, are there other advantages that you have accrued as a result of engaging differently? Had you not engaged differently with your customer, would you now be evolving from pre-opportunity into the opportunity phase and moving from *before* to *during* the sale?

Case Studies

Zurich Insurance Group

Zurich Insurance Group is a Switzerland-based global insurance company. With total business group volumes in excess of $74 billion (USD) and over 55,000 employees globally, Zurich provides a wide range of insurance products and services for individuals, small business, and mid-size and large companies, as well as multinationals. Zurich's Global Corporate team is a business unit within the larger Zurich umbrella that focuses on meeting the insurance and risk management needs of these large corporations and multinational companies. This global business unit within Zurich is composed of more than 3,500 employees and serves over 23,000 customers, delivering support in 210 countries and territories around the world. Global Corporate insures 86 percent of Fortune's Global 100 companies, and is the largest corporate business insurer in Europe and one of the two largest worldwide.

As a premium provider of risk management services and insurance products for their market segment, Zurich Global Corporate seeks to differentiate their offerings through a sharp focus on customer centricity and by delivering a superior customer experience. Global Corporate's go-to-market strategy is predicated upon the following:

- **Relationship management:** facilitating customer engagement with the right parties at the right time and expanding points of contact within both firms.

- **Underwriting transparency:** ensuring clarity and commonality in data analysis, which drives underwriting decisions, through direct dialogue with customers and brokers.

- **Risk insights:** turning data into insight and actionable awareness that helps the customer make better risk management decisions.

To assist with this strategy, Zurich has segmented its customer population and employed a customer relationship management model in the United States since 2002. They are the recognized industry leader in this space, offering a dedicated Global Relationship Leader (GRL) to select customers who fit a proprietary risk appetite-buying behavior model. These customers place a high value on Zurich's underwriting expertise, coordinated global claims service, and risk engineering, and their expectations include aligned international service networks capable of managing complex global insurance programs worldwide.

Zurich's customer relationship management model is the direct result of listening to customers. Thomas Hürlimann, CEO of Zurich's Global Corporate operation, provided context for Zurich's strategy:

"The strategy behind the development of our GRL model was to give corporate customers a single point of contact with knowledge and customer-engagement skills that can only be gained through years of wide-ranging insurance experience. Our ability to provide a global, differentiated customer experience by assigning a GRL to specific customers has helped us achieve higher retention as well as greater product density, along with Net Promoter® scores that reflect the positive experience we are delivering."

Customer Engagement: What Zurich Does to Effectively Engage Customers

Once a customer is formally segmented as a Relationship Customer within Zurich's program, a GRL is assigned. According to Valerie Butt, Global Head of Customer, Distribution and Market Development for Global Corporate, the next key step is for Zurich to establish a deep understanding of that customer, their industry segment, and their related approach to risk management. "As we evolved our GRL model, we wanted our GRLs to bring deep insights into our organization regarding our customers' business objectives, external drivers, and internal challenges," Butt explains. "By achieving this degree of customer understanding, we can create value that differentiates us from what our competitors offer. This becomes the logical path to being able to deliver unique value to our customers."

Zurich firmly believes that the key to success with this type of program is to look for opportunities to build relationships before the sale. "What's been essential for us is to first understand, and then embrace the fact that in corporate insurance, our customers only formally buy once a year per line of business risk," Butt adds. "By engaging customers when they are not in buying mode and offering pertinent risk insights, anticipating their future needs, and expanding our points of contact within their firm (and their related broker's firm), we are able to create customer value before the sale, sometimes even before there is even a thought of a sale."

Engagement Excellence: How Zurich Gets It Right for Customers

A prime example of the customer relationship management model at work can be found in a recent interaction between Cargill, one of the world's largest privately held companies (the largest in the United States), and Zurich. Cargill provides food, agriculture, and financial and industrial products and services to the world through its 143,000 employees in sixty-seven countries, and aspires to be the "global leader in nourishing people." The company also carries distinction as the largest grain exporter in the U.S. and the third largest meat and poultry processor.

As a Zurich Relationship Customer, Cargill is serviced by Zurich's GRL Matt Hoefert, who offers this insight:

"In the course of servicing Cargill, one of the challenges that I regularly explored was the global footprint of their operations and the resulting property insurance needs. Global property programs are extremely complex to administer and service, given the need to coordinate coverage and issue policies in multiple countries with multiple regulatory frameworks. Additional complexities include coordination and delivery of claims and risk engineering services for all major locations to ensure safe operations. Zurich's Multinational Insurance Proposition solution allows prompt response time and accurate transparency into the proper structuring of global placements. Cargill is impressed with our commitment to the resources that we deploy on their behalf, and our willingness to make our tools and technologies available to them."

Ultimately, under Hoefert's leadership, the Zurich team helped Cargill understand Zurich's global capabilities and resources, as well as how Zurich could customize its service response to fit Cargill's needs.

The Impact: Why Engagement Excellence Matters to Zurich's Customers

Zurich's "win" of the Cargill contract was merely the tip of the iceberg. As a result of Hoefert's proactive efforts, Zurich built a deep relationship with the company before the sale was ever finalized. Brian Turnwall, Cargill's Vice President of Global Insurance, describes the relationship this way:

"In my role, I'm exposed to multiple client executives who manage their firms' interactions with Cargill. Matt Hoefert stands out among these professionals based on his anticipation of key needs and challenges that my firm faces, combined with his consultative approach, strong project management skills, and persistence. I think Zurich's Global Relationship Leader model is the industry leading approach to insurer/customer engagement and a key reason I chose to do business with Zurich."

Cargill is just one of many examples of success that Zurich can attribute directly to their Customer Relationship Management program. Net Promoter relationship scores have improved for customers in the program, and Zurich's product density—the average number of discrete product lines placed per customer—for Relationship Customers is over eight lines of business per customer, as compared with an average product density of almost two lines of business for non-Relationship Customers.

The Takeaway: Why This Matters to You

The example of Zurich illustrates that the key to customer engagement before the sale is to know your customers well enough to anticipate their needs, and to proactively provide thought leadership by identifying potential solutions to assist with their business objectives and internal challenges before they are in buying mode. When this best practice is executed, you've not only earned the right to engage, but in the eyes of customer you may have already won, long before an RFP is ever issued.

In addition, this example indicates the importance of selecting the right customers, those who exhibit buying behaviors and needs that align with the core strengths of your products and services. By leveraging relationships with customers where you've created past proven value, you are in a better position to earn the right to grow and deepen the relationship between both organizations: before, during, and after the sale.

Author's Notes:

Total group business volumes comprises gross written premiums, policy fees, insurance deposits, and management fees generated within General Insurance, Global Life, and Farmers business segments of Zurich Insurance Group.

Net Promoter® is a registered trademark of Satmetrix Systems, Inc., Bain & Company, Inc., and Fred Reichheld, and is an index that measures customers' willingness to recommend a company's products or services to others.

Merck

Merck & Co. Inc., known as MSD (Merck Sharp & Dohme) outside of the U.S. and Canada, is an innovative global healthcare leader that is committed to improving health and well-being around the world. From developing new therapies that treat and prevent disease, to helping people in need, their passion for improving health keeps them at the forefront of scientific discovery and innovation in medicines, vaccines, biologic therapies, and animal health products. Current product categories include cardiovascular and respiratory health, diabetes, infectious disease, oncology, and women's health. With revenues in excess of $42 billion and operations in over 100 countries, Merck/MSD employs approximately 70,000 people globally.

While proud of past accomplishments, Merck is enthusiastic about the future and continues to focus research on areas of unmet need and expand on their strengths in areas like vaccines and biologics. With rapid transformation in the health care industry, however, pharmaceutical companies are bringing their medications into a very different marketplace. Customers are changing, customer needs are changing, healthcare delivery is more complex and requires more coordination, and rising costs are forcing payers to evaluate medical solutions in new and different ways.

As other healthcare organizations, such as national health systems, insurance companies, and integrated health delivery systems, make decisions about how to standardize care in a way that improves patient outcomes at a lower cost, individual physicians have less autonomy regarding the treatment of patients. At the same time, there is increasing consolidation among these healthcare organizations (for example, insurance company acquisitions and the integration of hospital systems and clinics), which has shifted market power to fewer decision makers. Many are Merck customers and they have become a necessary channel through which the company achieves its mission of improving health and well-being around the world. With an increased focus on population management to ensure appropriate levels of care across the full spectrum of patients, these customers require more collaborative and sophisticated levels of engagement.

Ken Frazier, Merck's Chairman of the Board and Chief Executive Officer, sees opportunity in these challenges:

"This is about changing the way that we approach customers, enhancing trust and moving away from a transactional relationship to a more strategic and longer term perspective. I believe that a deeper understanding of our top customers is the best path to achieving Merck's mission and growing our business. This will be a long-term, company-wide journey, one I am energized by and committed to because I am confident it will differentiate us and accelerate our growth strategy."

Customer Engagement: What Merck Does to Effectively Engage Customers

While customer focus has always been an integral part of Merck's culture, the traditional emphasis has been on understanding customers from a product-centric perspective. Shifting from transactional to more strategic, long-term relationships with their top customers meant that the company needed to take a different approach, to think outside-in and gain a deeper understanding of their customers. To accomplish this, they developed a customer-centric strategy that focuses on their top global and country-specific customers. Using strategic account management frameworks and capabilities, Merck's approach comprises the following:

- Outside-in differentiated insights.

- Openness to strategic, long-term, and mutually beneficial collaboration.

- Executive-level sponsorship and engagement.

- Dedicated Strategic Account Leaders (SALs) and appropriate customer account team resources that leverage the strength of the entire enterprise.

- Exploration of tailored, mutually beneficial co-creation initiatives and solutions.

To support global implementation, Merck developed a comprehensive toolkit and playbook, employing a five-stage process that begins with account selection and includes analyzing market trends, developing deep customer insight, engaging and aligning early with the customer on potential opportunity areas and joint aspirations, prioritizing initiatives, and developing initiative-level project plans.

One of Merck's strategic customers, Premier, Inc. is a health care performance improvement alliance of approximately 3,400 U.S. hospitals and 110,000 other providers. Their mission is simple: to improve the health of communities. Premier easily met Merck's "customer centricity" selection criteria, including strong leadership, progressive organizational mindset, financial and leadership stability, ethical business practices, leadership in the channel, active influence on and interest in healthcare reform, consistency with the mission with Merck, and openness to engagement.

As an industry leader, Premier's innovative technologies enable their members to collaborate more easily and efficiently. Premier's goal is to improve their members' quality outcomes, while safely reducing costs. By engaging members and revealing new opportunities, they empower the alliance to improve the performance of health care organizations and health care more broadly.

Muna Bhanji, Merck's executive sponsor for Premier, offers this perspective:

"Our engagement with Premier is continuous, cross-enterprise, and maintains a long-term view. Trust, accountability, and commitment across both organizations have been strengthened; each organization is enriched by a deeper understanding of where there may be areas of mutual benefit. The dialogue regarding alignment across organizations, or a lack of alignment and the reasons why, is open and candid. When the level of trust and engagement is this high, both sides lean in to see what could be possible and then come together to make it happen."

Engagement Excellence: How Merck Gets It Right for Customers

Over the years, Premier has by and large provided positive feedback on doing business with Merck, but they lacked confidence in Merck's ability to consistently deliver on promises. With a new focus on customer centricity, Merck asked Denise Juliano, a long-term employee with extensive experience in sales, marketing, and management, to take the reins as Strategic Account Leader (SAL) for Premier.

After studying Premier's business in-depth, Juliano engaged resources across the organization and ensured that every Merck team member understood Premier's business and their role in the engagement. Juliano says:

> "I'm the steward of the customer at all times. It's my job to engage the organization, enable everyone to lead with their expertise, and hold them accountable. It's critically important that we come to the table with a good understanding of Premier's agenda and how it aligns with Merck's. When two organizations do something new and innovative, you have to pave the road as you drive on it. When you're interacting differently, one of the biggest challenges is that you're learning together as you go."

Based on each company's business imperatives, Merck and Premier mapped out areas of strategic alignment and identified opportunities for both short- and long-term potential collaboration. The success with early initiatives has significantly improved Premier's confidence in Merck's ability to deliver. Juliano explains:

> "Premier works with between 1,100 and 2,000 suppliers. Before, Premier couldn't pick Merck out of a line-up and now we are one of their top three. How did it happen? Over time, we built a trusted and transparent relationship with Premier that resulted in a differentiated

perception of Merck. Because we are collaborating across divisions, and because we are actively working together on creating innovative solutions to big industry challenges, Merck is top of mind when they are considering who to partner with in any given area. We're working together to identify potential population health management solutions to enable positive patient outcomes. If we can successfully co-create and commercialize solutions, it will bring value to patients, Premier's customers, Merck's customers, Premier, and Merck."

The Impact: Why Engagement Excellence Matters to Merck's Customers

Premier acknowledges the value that Merck's customer centricity strategy has brought to their interactions and their ability to jointly improve health and well-being. David Edwards, Premier's Senior Vice President of Supplier Relations, observes:

> "Our relationship with Merck/MSD has changed dramatically over the last year. We have a quarterback in Denise Juliano who proactively seeks alignment and opportunities for collaboration, and finds ways to solve problems of mutual interest. She looks at Merck's products, depth, resources, people, and talent, and matches them up with Premier's resources and talent against a common goal. She's constantly trying to find ways to bring us together in a unified way where 1 + 1 = 7.
>
> Combining the two organizations' strengths has had a faster and greater impact than either one could have on its own. The theme is that we're stronger together. I credit Denise for being decisive in finding common areas where we complement one another."

The Takeaway: Why This Matters to You

Merck's customer-centric approach demonstrates the power of trust-based, collaborative partnerships in a rapidly evolving industry. By developing a deep understanding of the customer's business, aligning objectives, and engaging the expertise of cross-functional resources, Merck is able to explore innovative healthcare solutions with their top customers long before a specific opportunity has been identified.

Merck believes this proactive collaboration before, during, and after engagement on any specific project is mutually beneficial to both companies and empowers everyone to achieve their shared vision of improved health and well-being worldwide.

BNY Mellon

Headquartered in New York City's bustling financial district, BNY Mellon is a global investments company dedicated to helping its clients manage and service their financial assets throughout the entire investment life-cycle. Started by Alexander Hamilton in 1784, BNY Mellon is one of the most enduring financial institutions in the world, innovating and prospering through every economic event and market move over the past 230 years.

With over 50,000 employees worldwide, BNY Mellon can serve as a single point of contact for clients looking to create, trade, hold, manage, service, distribute, or restructure their investments. Whether providing financial services for institutions, corporations, or individual investors, BNY Mellon delivers informed investment management and investment services in thirty-five countries and more than 100 markets. As of June 30, 2015, BNY Mellon had $28.6 trillion in assets under custody and/or administration, and $1.7 trillion in assets under management.

The company's Global Client Management (GCM) division is responsible for creating, building, and deepening relationships with the Bank's largest and most complex global clients. The priority for BNY Mellon and its GCM team is to apply a deep knowledge of clients, their markets, and their industries to deliver innovative solutions tailored to meet their present and future needs. In doing so, BNY Mellon strives to be a strategic partner focused on helping clients succeed.

Karen Peetz, President of BNY Mellon and the executive sponsor of the GCM team, offers this insight: "We are extremely proud of the client relationships that we have developed over the years, yet we believed we could do even more in order to be a strategic partner—not just a provider." She adds, "Keys to this are aligning internal partners first and then bringing them together to collaborate on the development and execution of innovative solutions that benefit both the client and our overall relationship."

Customer Engagement: What BNY Mellon Does to Effectively Engage Customers

Committed to more effective "strategic partnering," a subset of the GCM team was selected to pilot a "high-touch" relationship management approach with a select group of the firm's clients. Among them were some of the world's largest financial institutions and corporations, including global banks, asset managers, and insurance companies. Objectives of the pilot included ensuring that BNY Mellon had a strong understanding of each client's industry, corporate objectives, and challenges, thus establishing a foundation for greater levels of client collaboration around new opportunities to leverage BNY Mellon's broad and deep portfolio of investment solutions.

Based on positive client feedback throughout the pilot, this new approach has since been expanded to include all client relationships managed by GCM. At the same time, the GCM team has been reorganized into key industry segments, further aligning the expertise of BNY Mellon's resources with clients. GCM teams have been provided with strategic account management and planning training, equipping them with best practices to grow strategic client relationships.

Executive Vice President Fred Bromberg leads a team that supports global financial institutions. One client that his team focuses on is a global banking and financial services organization with a significant presence in retail banking and brokerage, consumer and commercial banking, mortgage lending, and investment banking. For this particular client, Bromberg and his team set out to develop an account plan with the specific goal of evolving the nature of the relationship from more tactical to more collaborative and strategic.

To launch their efforts, Bromberg brought together an extended team of people within BNY Mellon who were associated with the client. This team included GCM team members, as well as key individuals with client-facing roles within the various BNY Mellon businesses. Together, they discussed and explored the client relationship, carefully evaluating the core business that existed, as well as those areas that represented the greatest potential for growth.

Regarding the importance of heightened levels of collaboration in growing this relationship, Bromberg offers this perspective:

"What we found through this process is that the catalysts to deepening the strategic partnership were our counterparts within the client's global markets and investment banking divisions. They were able to broker introductions and help our team navigate the complexities of their institution. Further, we successfully identified executive sponsors within both firms to help drive a mutually beneficial partnership."

Engagement Excellence: How BNY Mellon Gets It Right for Customers

Beginning before the sale with research, collaboration, and fact-finding to better understand the client's business, the BNY Mellon team completed its analysis, developing an initial strategic agenda of potential possibilities to explore with the client. Then, using the account planning process, they validated and prioritized these potential areas of value creation with the client. With client support, the BNY Mellon team was then able to take deliberate steps to build upon the current relationship, dramatically enhancing the client's perception of their relationship.

By working more collaboratively together, the BNY Mellon team was able to identify and vision a number of potential opportunities with their client that had not yet been realized. Then, by engaging effectively, the Bank became strategically positioned to help the client successfully achieve key objectives, which included improving operational efficiency and balance sheet optimization, as well as identifying best-in-class products for its brokerage clientele. Additionally, the BNY Mellon team was able to expand its opportunity to partner with the client by exploring other keys areas of potential client value creation, such as trade execution, capital markets, and advisory services.

Throughout this process, the BNY Mellon team introduced client team members to new contacts within BNY Mellon that would be directly involved in considering the client's top business "asks," or partnership requests. This greater transparency helped position the client for easier access to the individuals that would make these decisions, driving even greater levels of collaboration between the two organizations. Finally, by creating a platform for mutual business growth, BNY Mellon further reinforced its commitment to deepening the current relationship and delivering innovative solutions to address the client's needs.

The Impact: Why Engagement Excellence Matters to BNY Mellon's Customers

With the mutually agreed upon client value targets serving as a roadmap for growth, BNY Mellon developed a strategic partnership with this client by delivering creative solutions that aligned with the client's external drivers, business objectives, and internal challenges. Even before putting a strategic plan in place to facilitate growth and innovation, the Bank provided a variety of solutions and services to the client. But since the development and implementation of a strategic vison and mutual plan, BNY Mellon has successfully expanded the value that it delivers to the client into a number of significant new areas.

The BNY Mellon team continues to focus on the client's business asks, making connections with the right people within BNY Mellon, and advocating for the client on business proposals that make economic sense for both parties. Current discussions include how BNY Mellon's technology advances and strategic plans can provide additional benefits to the client in the years to come, clear evidence of the elevated dialogue that has resulted from excellent client engagement. BNY Mellon expects to further expand their relationship with this client to address additional opportunities identified as part of the strategic account planning process.

The Takeaway: Why This Matters to You

It's difficult, if not impossible, to align effectively with a client if you are not aligned internally, within your own organization. Realizing this, Bromberg invested the effort to reach out to his internal colleagues and stakeholders and engaged them in his plan for client growth and success, involving them in defining the following objectives for the client:

- Deepening senior-level access to reinforce BNY Mellon as a trusted advisor to the client.

- Collaborating internally with the entire global team to effectively deliver BNY Mellon as "one company."

- Leveraging BNY Mellon Executive Committee members to demonstrate full alignment with the strategic growth plan for this client.

Paul Sari, Managing Director of BNY Mellon Investment Management, is one of these stakeholders, and he offers this insight: "In an environment of enhanced global presence, ever-changing regulations, and the need to continue to evolve and grow as a business, having a trusted strategic partner that is in it with you for the long-term is a key to success." Recognizing the value of this partnership, Sari and the other members of the BNY Mellon team are closely aligned with Bromberg and his GCM team members on behalf of this client.

BNY Mellon believes this client relationship has developed from being a "provider of choice" into a long-term strategic partnership, which will benefit both organizations. By focusing on the relationship and the client's needs before pursuing specific opportunities, the outcome can be that both organizations achieve their strategic priorities by supporting their mutual growth efforts. BNY Mellon's approach is to engage effectively with clients, before, during, and long after each sale has been made.

II

Win: Driving Success During the Sale

Discover the Drivers: Understanding What's at Stake for Your Customers

IN SECTION I, we looked at how to achieve success before the sale. We examined how to do your homework and become a student of the customer, and then how to put this knowledge to work by selecting the right possibilities to explore, giving the customer a reason to engage with you. We described how to help your customer build a vision of success by focusing on how they define value, and explained how to use the information and insight that you now have assimilated to elevate the conversation through the development of customer value targets.

Your successful customer engagement efforts have helped you evolve from pre-opportunity into an active sales opportunity, and your focus has shifted from *before* to *during* the sale. Now, in Section II, we discuss extending and expanding your research, exploration, visioning, and elevation into a well-defined opportunity, putting you in a position to innovate with your customer and consider new ways to create and co-create value. When you engage this way, you'll find that it's less noisy and congested with competitors, which is exactly where you want to be when you're planning to win. We begin by focusing on the strategy of discovery.

What Is Discovery?

Discovery is the process of understanding your customer's business. It involves gaining a thorough understanding of the external drivers compelling your customer to act, the business objectives that represent how they intend to address those drivers, and the internal challenges that could prevent them from achieving their objectives. This involves asking value-focused questions that provide insight into those drivers and objectives, as well as into their internal challenges and personal success criteria.

Discovery is perpetual. It's a process without an end, especially in a customer relationship that you want to keep, because as you continue to invest time and learn about your customer, the result is stronger mutual engagement. As your knowledge becomes deeper and broader, you earn the right to ask questions about other, previously unexplored areas. Your credibility grows as your understanding of your customer's business expands.

What does it mean to understand the customer's business? You're probably familiar with the dynamic nature of understanding. Haven't we all had the experience of thinking, "Yes, I've got it!" only to discover that we didn't get it at all? Or maybe we did get it, but something changed, and now we don't anymore. Understanding your customer's business is like that. You can understand it somewhat, or understand some part of it, but you simply can't expect to get it like your customer does. Admittedly, we have all thought at some point, "Hey, I probably know as much about my customer's business as they do." We were kidding ourselves.

So if you can't possibly know all that your customer knows, why bother with discovery? Jonathan Farrington, the senior partner at Jonathan Farrington & Associates and CEO of Top Sales World, offers this perspective: "Discovery allows us to demonstrate our credibility, knowledge, and commercial bandwidth—'Before I attempt to sell to you, I will show you that I understand your precise requirements.' Frontline sales professionals who are able to manage this stage well are better able to upgrade their status from a 'me also' supplier to an 'only me' one."

Because discovery is more than just an exercise, understanding the customer gives you the ability to do some very important things:

- **Establish credibility and build a trust-based relationship**. Customers want to deal with suppliers that are credible. They want relationships based on trust. And they want to affiliate with someone who really understands their business.

- **Propose a solution that fits.** When you understand what your customer is trying to do and are able to help them recognize how your solution specifically connects to what they consider important, you can create a sense of fit that is very powerful. You can't do that if you don't understand what their challenges are.

- **Prove that you can deliver value.** You can be specific, because you know what their external drivers and business objectives are. You can show them how your solution fits and how you can help them be successful.

- **Gain the competitive advantage**. When you know more about the customer than your competitors do, you have a better chance of winning their business. You can rise above the clamor and have conversations that no one else is having because you are further elevating a dialogue that was initiated earlier.

Through discovery, you seek to see the as-yet unseen. This quest extends beyond what you don't already know; in many cases, you'll be able to discover what your competitors have not yet seen, and in some cases, things that even your customer has yet to see.

The "Value" of the Value-Focused Question

If understanding your customer's business is what you need to do, then asking the right questions is how you do it. You're probably thinking, "Why wouldn't I ask the right questions?" It might be better to ask, "How do I know if I'm asking the right questions?"

Too many questions asked by salespeople tend to be technical in nature, most likely because customer-facing professionals receive considerably more training about the products they sell than about the value those products provide to their customers. But asking questions intended to discover something data- or fact-related (for example, "When do you plan to make a decision? How many employees will be impacted? What type of budget is in place to support this project?") can provide a false sense of security. While these types of inquiries may be necessary and helpful, they can also be too focused and, therefore, extremely limiting.

A *value-focused question*, on the other hand, provides an understanding of the customer's business that moves you into the realm of "how." An effective value-focused question is designed to help you gain information and insight, and lead to awareness that will ultimately have value to both you and your customer. Questions such as "When you look out over the next 12 months, how would you describe some of the most important objectives that you and your team must accomplish?" and "If my organization were to work closely with you and your team in pursuit of this opportunity, how would you measure our success or effectiveness together upon completion of the project?" can go a long way in helping you focus on what's most important to your customer. As you get better at asking value-focused questions, you learn that you don't have to ask as many to get the insight and awareness that you need.

A quick Internet search yields hundreds of book titles that discuss how to ask questions—open-ended questions, closing questions, power questions, etc. You are probably familiar with most of these concepts. Practically speaking, however, it's clear that many salespeople and account managers simply aren't as good at asking the right questions as they should be.

For your customer, the value is in providing information that can bring your proposal into greater alignment with their needs and requirements. If your customer never says, "Here's my world; these are my pressure points," it's unrealistic to expect that you can align your solution with what they consider to be most important. While some customers may be able to convey their needs generally through RFPs, many are less effective at expressing precisely what they need *and* what they want. Clearly, the customer benefits when their most important suppliers understand their needs, requirements, and wants.

As a supplier, the value for you is in establishing a powerful and unique collaborative platform for the exchange of ideas. Asking value-focused questions can help you rise above vendor status and ascend to a level that is less crowded and more collaborative. When you approach discovery as nothing more than a data exchange, you miss an opportunity, because data is only a part of the emerging picture. Discovery is ultimately about gaining the insight and awareness that strengthens the foundation of the relationship in the areas of trust and credibility.

In a collaborative environment, the right kind of sharing can have an extraordinary impact on business. By helping your customer sculpt their vision into something well defined, tangible, and achievable, you put yourself in a position to innovate together and open new avenues of discussion for the creation and co-creation of value.

The Quest for Actionable Awareness

The last time you asked your customer a question, did their answer provide any information or insight that you could use? If so, did you do anything with what you learned?

Actionable awareness is the final stage of refinement and prioritization. It's where data is evolved into information, and information is evolved into insight. This takes insight to a level at which salespeople and account managers can actually do something with it. It's what's left after three levels of "filtration," as Figure 5-1 shows.

The first filter involves distilling down the *data*, often lots of it, to some level of relevant *information*. The second filter involves examining and further reducing the information to provide meaningful *insight* into the customer and their business. The third (and most underutilized) level of filtration involves prioritizing the insights you have captured into areas of awareness where you and your team can and will take action. Your effective discovery efforts will equip you not only with the awareness of knowing what to do, but also with ideas about how you can most effectively do it. And in a competitive selling situation, this is a very powerful position in which to find yourself.

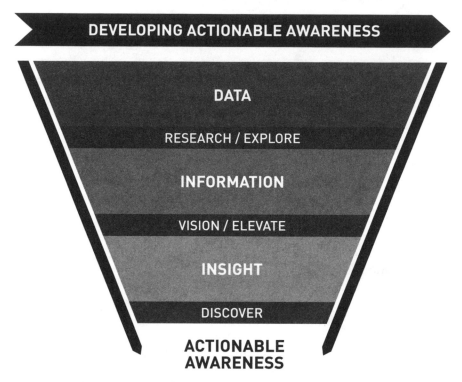

Figure 5-1. **Developing actionable awareness.**

Some of the exchanges between you and your customer may be casual. They are likely to include questions that do little more than keep everyone talking. Cordial enough, these interactions may reveal something interesting, but what you really want is the kind of information that will take you to the next level of engagement. The purist might say that any information from a customer is helpful, but the time to research and explore anything and everything was earlier. Now you're on a purposeful mission for some very specific insights, which will ultimately lead to actionable awareness. With time in short supply, why waste a single moment asking about something that isn't critical when you could be asking a question with far greater potential value to both you and your customer?

Living in the age of big data, it can be easy to confuse an abundance of information with a real understanding of your customer's business. Coming from the information technology industry, we understand the appeal around the concept of big data, but as a practical matter, we also know that big data doesn't equal big information or big insight. And it absolutely does not equal actionable awareness.

Value-focused questions lead you beyond data, information, and insight so you can take the appropriate action on your customer's behalf. This happens because you are able to recognize what is important and what isn't. Value-focused questions help your customer understand that your actions are based on an authentic desire to ensure their success. This is the power of actionable awareness.

If you have ever participated in an account or opportunity review, you probably saw some of your organization's account team members or managers make a lengthy presentation about an important customer. Did they just offer up the kind of data that is easily available through the Internet, or did they provide usable information on how to grow the account, the past proven value that had been created and co-created throughout the relationship, the competitors that are also vying for your customer's business, or their vision for expanding the relationship to the next level? Did they mention how and why they were going to develop and win new business, or discuss any significant obstacles that would need to be removed in order to do so?

It's human nature to latch on to data, but data should never be mistaken for insight, much less actionable awareness. As companies make massive investments in their efforts to generate and provide information to their sales, account management, and customer service professionals, it is wise to take a step back and determine how much of it will ever translate into something truly actionable.

The quest for actionable awareness is built on a simple concept—empowering salespeople, account managers, and their teams to rise above the plethora of data and information so that they acquire the awareness that leads to the actions that result in customer value creation and co-creation.

The Focus of Your Discovery Efforts

Suppliers overwhelmingly spend more time talking about their own offerings than about what's of value to their customers. Whenever you're engaging with a customer, the focus of your discovery efforts should be on what's important to the customer, not on your product, its features, and the alleged benefits.

What Does Your Customer Want to Talk About? Think of a recent conversation you had with a customer who was clearly engaged in everything that was being said. Why were they so attentive? Perhaps they were highly fascinated by your compelling description of your offerings, but it's more likely that you were talking about their organization and the things that mean the most to them.

When your goal is actionable awareness, you should first seek to understand what your customer cares about. Practical, real-world experience has taught us that these topics typically fall into the four general categories shown in Figure 5-2.

> ## UNDERSTAND WHAT MATTERS MOST TO YOUR CUSTOMER

Their External Drivers	What external drivers and pressures are impacting your customer's business?
Their Business Objectives	What is your customer doing to address their external drivers?
Their Internal Challenges	What could prevent your customer from meeting their business objectives?
Their Success Criteria	How will success be defined for each member of your customer's decision team?

Figure 5-2. Understand what matters most to your customer.

External Drivers. *What factors outside of your customer's control are impacting their business and putting pressure on them to take action?* A conversation about your customer's external drivers is an opportunity to establish credibility by demonstrating that you have done your homework and gained at least some knowledge of their business and environment. Your understanding of what is putting pressure on the customer is typically the first step to developing actionable awareness.

A customer's external drivers, which can be positive or negative, might include the following:

- **Competition.** Does your customer have a competitor that is launching a new product? Making an important acquisition? Shutting down a facility?

- **Customers.** Customers are buying differently these days. Their customers are, too. In many cases, your customer's customers are their most compelling driver.

- **Government.** Most businesses are impacted by government in some way, whether it's changing policies, reduced funding, or new regulations. Administrations change. Political alignments shift.

- **Economy.** In the wake of the recession, it's clear that economic conditions impact how businesses operate and plan for the future. Outside of your customer's control, the economy can be a significant driver—positive or negative.

- **Regulation.** Regulated industries operate in complex environments where the unpredictability of constantly evolving rules, compliance, and reporting can have a tremendous impact. Does your customer operate within a highly-regulated industry?

- **Technology.** Whenever companies such as Microsoft, Apple, and Google release new operating systems or software, the providers of supporting hardware and devices feel the ripple effect. How does changing technology impact your customer?

- **Shareholders.** A company's owners can exert a significant influence, particularly when they are not satisfied. This type of driver exerts a pressure that typically requires a sense of urgency to take action sooner rather than later.

Business Objectives. *What is your customer doing to address their external drivers?* Most people grappling with conditions beyond their control begin with the question, "Am I going to do anything about this or not?" A business objective is the customer's planned response to the impact, or potential impact, of a driver. A savvy supplier's goal is to discover what the customer plans to do, and then align and connect with those business objectives.

In the end, customer value is typically a function of revenue and cost, so organizations look for the ultimate value that a purchase of goods or services will provide them. As they consider whether or not to pursue an opportunity, they generally ask, "Can I generate revenue if I do this?" Then, "How much do I have to spend?" in order to make it happen.

When the cost of taking action exceeds the revenue benefits, it is less likely that the customer will put a plan into place. Objectives on the cost-reduction side, such as improving product quality or reducing time-to-market, may seem clear and straightforward at first glance, but analyses of return on investment (ROI) and total cost of ownership (TCO) may leave the customer convinced that the "juice isn't worth the squeeze" or that the cost of taking action isn't practical.

Examples of business objectives include the following:

- **Revenue.** To bring in new revenues, your customer plans to offer a new product or service. Ultimately, they will measure the value of meeting this objective in terms of the costs they incur to put the product on the market or to implement the new service, offset by the revenue that results.

- **Cost.** Some business objectives exist purely on the cost side— consolidating suppliers, for example. Customers sometimes complain that managing too many relationships with potential providers is overwhelming, and that reducing suppliers will increase their efficiency. They can also use this to negotiate better contracts with suppliers that fear being left out.

- **Risk reduction.** Customers that make buying decisions based on their perception of reduced business risk might spend more with a particular supplier for a less-than-ideal solution because they believe that the supplier reduces their exposure to a range of risks.

It's critically important for your customer to understand that the risk of investing in your product or service is significantly less than the risk you'll be helping them minimize or remove from their business.

A customer's business objectives that involve taking risk out of the business can sometimes trump revenue and cost objectives. The more competent, credible, and trustworthy you are, the less risk your customer is likely to perceive in doing business with you.

Ultimately, you should look at ways to help your customer drive revenues up, bring costs down, and reduce risk; sometimes you can accomplish all three. When you bring knowledge, best practices, insight, and especially actionable awareness to your customer, you stand tall among your competitors, and elevate your customer conversations even further.

Internal Challenges. *What can prevent your customer from meeting their business objectives?* A customer is most likely to pick up the phone and talk to you when there's a problem. They may not have enough time or resources. They may have time and resources, but not enough expertise. Whatever the case may be, they've bumped into a problem, need help, and want to talk with you. Internal challenges are the problems, obstacles, hurdles, potholes, and blocking factors that are confronting your customer as they attempt to press forward with their objectives and plans, and discovering those challenges means uncovering potential areas of value creation and co-creation for you and your organization.

Success Criteria. *What will cause your customer to be successful?* When was the last time you asked a customer point-blank what success looks like for them as an individual? If you don't know the customer well, it's likely you haven't yet earned the right, so the question may not apply to less developed relationships, but at some point in the future this question will apply. Success to a particular individual on a personal level may be dramatically different from the organization's definition of success.

To initiate this conversation, consider asking your customer, "What are the most important objectives you are pursuing today, and what do you need to accomplish in order to achieve them?" The customer may be reaching for multiple objectives, and might need a supplier to partner with. Or your contacts may have teams they have to satisfy, bosses whose objectives must be met, or career goals that they are pursuing. Unless you ask, you won't know.

It's extremely valuable to your customer to know that you understand what's at stake for them. If you can align with that, you have something powerful. If you are the only supplier to make this discovery, then you also have a competitive advantage.

Keep in mind that your customer has a business plan, either formal or informal, that they are working to execute. Departmental or line-of-business plans typically roll up into the corporate plan, and you should make it a priority to understand as much as possible about what they must accomplish at different levels of their business. This means paying careful attention to the specific success criteria and measurements that impact the people with whom you are engaging.

Connecting your solutions and value specifically to the customer's challenges and objectives is powerful, and can make the difference between winning and losing.

What Else Can Be Discovered if You Ask the Right Value-Focused Questions? Discovery is by no means limited to the areas we just covered. Through your effective discovery efforts, you can also learn more.

Your Customer's Background and History. *Where has the customer been, and who have they been there with?* Do you or your company have history with this customer? Is it positive? How do you get to that historical information? A CRM solution may enable you to discover your organization's prior experience with the customer, but alone, it's unlikely to be enough.

Much customer research can be done without ever leaving your office. The Internet, certain technologies (such as InsideView and LinkedIn), and other social media offer quick and easy access to a wealth of information that would have been considerably harder to come by just a few years ago. With some practice, you can determine which social media channels are best for monitoring your customers, as well as the industries into which their customers are selling. Newsworthy developments, acquisitions and mergers, governmental regulations, and other trigger events can each be considered as a potential reason to reach out to an existing or new customer.

Internal collaboration is also important, because it fosters a team approach. You might be surprised to discover how much your colleague in the next office, or on the other side of the world, knows about your customer. Tribal knowledge, or an organization's unwritten information, can yield helpful knowledge. You just need to ask.

Also consider the landscape or footprint of your company's business across your customer's organization. When you consider how much your customer spends with all of the providers in your market, it's important to note your portion of their overall spend, which is sometimes referred to as "wallet share." But your percentage of the customer's business is only part of your consideration: What are you providing to your customer, and where within their organization (across business units and regions) are you providing it? By interpreting the answers to these questions, you can begin to paint the picture of where you are, where you aren't, and where you can grow your business with the customer. It's always a good idea to know where there is potential to increase your share of the customer's spend in your market, and you have to assume that your competitor is trying to do the same.

Your Customer's Requirements and the Scope of Opportunity. *What is your customer trying to accomplish in order to successfully address their drivers, achieve their objectives, and meet their challenges?* Is their vision of success fixed or expandable? RFP documents may reveal some of this information, but once requirements have been put into writing it's probably too late to engage the customer directly for discovery purposes, much less to have any additional influence on them. As we discussed in Strategy 3, some of the most powerful visioning takes place when you are initially engaging with your customer, because the earlier you're involved in these types of conversations, the more influence you can have on RFP requirements. Does the customer want to talk about innovation? Are they looking to expand their vision? Is there an opportunity for value co-creation? It's better to do your discovery before the RFP is issued, because once it hits the street, you're too late.

The Competitive Landscape. *What is your customer's competitive land-scape?* You have to be fairly close to a customer to get this kind of information, and it has to be culturally acceptable to pursue these types of questions. But sometimes it's perfectly appropriate and comfortable to say, "If you don't mind my asking, what kinds of providers are you considering?" and "Can you tell me who else is involved in this process?" If you can stay within the customer's comfort zone, you should be able to find out who's in, who's out, and who's trying to get in, as well as their respective track records with the customer. You can also discover whether any competing suppliers consider the customer to be a strategic account. If so, you can expect that some work has been done, both before this sale and after their last.

Your Customer's Decision Criteria, Process, and Team. *What criteria will have the greatest impact on your customer's decision?* What process is in place for the customer to make a decision and reach a consensus? Who are the decision team participants and at what levels do they weigh in? Who are the influencers? The recommenders? The decision makers? The approvers? How have prior decisions been made?

Conventional sales wisdom has routinely advised against spending time with people who do not have the authority to say yes, or who are not in a position to make the decision to buy. We disagree. Instead, we urge you to remember that someone who can't say yes may still be able to say no. They may not be making the decision themselves, but they could be making a recommendation to the person who is.

It's important to do discovery at all levels of the customer's organization, not just at the top. Senior executives today are more challenged with information complexity and time management issues than ever before. Many are being asked to make decisions about things they don't fully understand. Where do they go to do their own discovery? They ask middle managers or individual contributors/subject matter experts (SMEs) for help and support about a specific topic. There's nothing wrong with that. In fact, it's an example of effective organizational alignment. And when this happens, you'll be very happy that you've done your discovery both inside and outside the "decision suite."

Are You Asking the Right Questions of the Right People, Listening to What Your Customer Is Saying, and (Really) Hearing What They're Telling You? No matter how good your questions (and your ability to ask them) are, your discovery efforts will fail if you don't actually hear what the customer tells you. Effective discovery requires you to be deliberate about the following:

- **Asking the right questions of the right people.** Each person you speak with has a different area of focus. People at higher levels typically focus on the whole company or organization. Middle managers are more interested in their business unit, division, or department. Individual contributors or SMEs tend to concentrate on their specific project or area of expertise. It's important to develop questions that are appropriate to the individuals you are engaging with, and interesting to them based on their level and perspective.

- **Listening to what they are saying (and not saying).** What is not said can be as important as what is stated outright. Take heed of the unspoken, because your customer may not be comfortable or prepared to talk about something significant. It may be a timing issue, or they may feel that you haven't earned the right. Or perhaps they are testing you to learn whether you have invested the time and effort they require to consider you credible and trustworthy.

- **Hearing what they tell you.** When your customer responds to a question, it helps if they "see you listen" to their answer. When you take notes or repeat back a summary of what they just said and ask them to verify your understanding, they quite literally see you hear them.

- **Separating the important few from the unimportant many.** A key component of *really hearing* is developing a knack for quickly sifting through data to evolve information into insight, and then into actionable awareness.

- **Trusting, but verifying.** Important questions must be asked, and you have to listen to and validate the answers during discovery. By doing so, you can be more certain that what you are hearing from the customer is factual and complete.

Most people are not as good at listening as they think they are. We're all so accustomed to passive listening that we simply don't hear what's actually being said. One executive recently articulated frustration with her people who don't hear the customer because they're too busy "waiting to talk." Think about that. A customer you're meeting with says something that you'd like to respond to. You don't interrupt, but you are poised to speak up as soon as they finish. You aren't taking in what they're saying; you're no longer hearing much of anything, because you're too busy waiting to talk. Even the most attentive listener can find it challenging to absorb information, but when you're busy with your own thoughts, you're likely to come away from the meeting with much less than you would have if you were listening intently.

We recommend that you invest the time to prepare effective discovery questions in advance of your customer meetings. Time and time again, we have heard highly experienced salespeople and account managers express regret because they hadn't asked a customer a specific question, and it's too late for a do-over.

Here are a few examples of questions that might be helpful to you in your discovery efforts. Remember that you should always tailor your questions to your customer, and feel comfortable with those questions before you ask:

- **External drivers:** "I read in your last 10-K that new Food and Drug Administration regulations have significantly increased your labor costs. What other external influences are putting pressure on your business?"

- **Business objectives:** "Other than hiring and providing people with the right training and tools, what types of objectives or plans are being put in place to address these drivers?"

- **Internal challenges:** "As you attempt to equip and enable people with training and tools, what potential problems or obstacles could prevent you from meeting this objective?"

- **Success criteria:** "Why is it important to you and your organization's success to address these drivers, meet your objectives, and resolve your challenges?"

By all means, plan your discovery efforts carefully. But be ready for surprises and willing to be flexible and adaptive. Your "in the moment" discovery can help you achieve a level of alignment that will be instrumental in winning the business and advancing a key relationship.

Testing the Effectiveness of Your Discovery

The following six sets of questions will help you determine whether your discovery has been effective:

1. **Have you identified your customer's external drivers and pressures?** What are they? Has your customer confirmed them?

2. **Have you identified your customer's business objectives and plans to address their drivers and pressures?** What are they? Has your customer confirmed them?

3. **Have you identified your customer's internal challenges and obstacles?** What are they? Has your customer confirmed them?

4. **Have you identified your customer's decision criteria, decision process, and the key members of their decision team?** Who are

they? Who are the influencers? What are the internal politics and dynamics within the decision team? Based on potential final outcomes, who "wins" and who "loses?"

5. **Have you identified the obstacles and risks associated with proceeding (or not proceeding) with this opportunity?** What are they? What will it cost the customer to do nothing?

6. **Have you confirmed that your customer has executive-level commitment to this opportunity?** Who is committed? Why? Have you identified any potential customer sponsors and supporters for you and your organization?

STRATEGY 6

Align the Teams: Developing Customer Sponsors and Supporters

IF THE GOAL of discovery is to equip you with actionable awareness of your customer's external drivers, business objectives, and internal challenges, then alignment puts this awareness to work developing value-focused relationships with your customer's team. This means more than simply making connections and developing new contacts.

In the earlier phases of your engagement with the customer, you worked to establish credibility and build trust. By asking the right questions, you elevated the dialogue and learned how your customer defines success. You did your research, explored possibilities, built a vision of their success, and elevated the conversation—all by working together. Your customer knows you're authentic because you've taken the time to understand what's important to them. You've earned the right to align.

Many Are Connected; Few Are Truly Aligned

We define alignment as connecting and integrating resources with the customer's team, and building relationships based on trust, credibility, and value creation. Always intentional, never accidental, alignment is a powerful component of effective customer engagement and the bridge between the discovery process and the proactive positioning of your solutions and their value to your customer. It's the one element that weaves its way through every facet of the *Engage/Win/Grow* approach.

Let's be clear—not everyone agrees. Some sales training and consulting firms suggest that there is little time to build and grow authentic relationships in today's business environment, and that if you just make good use of their sales process and fill out their forms, then good things will happen: sales will close and customers will be happy. This is not a plan to win.

Relationships matter more than ever. In today's challenging business environment, most customers are stressed, pressed for results, and under duress to make things happen within their organizations—and to do so under conditions that can be formidable. Customers regularly tell us that they are expected to deliver results and meet objectives in unrealistically tight time frames, which means they have to ask their suppliers to do the same. In this demanding climate, customers want to work with providers they can trust and count on to deliver. Their success, and perhaps even their jobs, depend on it.

With the exception of an occasional commodity business, remarkably few of the clients and customers we've interviewed have even hinted that relationships do not factor into their buying decisions. It matters that your customer's team members find you credible. It matters that they find you trustworthy. And it matters that they see you focused on their success rather than on a quick sale.

If effective discovery is the key that unlocks the door to value creation and co-creation, then it's your alignment with the customer that swings that door wide open.

Why do certain customers and their suppliers align while others don't? This calls for a bit of introspection. Think of a time when you found yourself in close alignment with your customer. Now ask yourself why it happened. Alignment may be initiated based on common interests or perspectives, but it likely wouldn't have endured unless both you and your customer had an opportunity and a desire to create or co-create value together.

Misalignment will cause you to fail in your efforts to effectively equip yourself to move into the next phases of *Engage/Win/Grow*. Over the years, we've observed repeatedly that suppliers who actively pursue alignment with their customers enjoy competitive advantage.

Can alignment occur without proper discovery? Maybe, but why leave something so important to chance? As a successful salesperson, you need something to align with, and your discovery has revealed what's important to the customer. This is your opportunity to prove that you have listened, and just as importantly, that you have heard what the customer is telling you. When you demonstrate your understanding of what they really care about, you can further elevate the conversation as you extend your actionable awareness to what they consider most important. You can't do this without deliberate, proactive, and effective discovery.

The Dimensions of Alignment

From observing customer/supplier relationships, we've developed a list of the five key areas where you're most likely to find alignment in action:

1. **Relationships:** Top-performing sales professionals consistently demonstrate an ability to build and grow strong trust-based relationships with their customers. Relationships are a critical component of effective customer engagement.

2. **Solutions:** Successful salespeople provide solutions to address customer challenges, problems, opportunities, or issues. These solutions typically include products, resources, expertise, services, industry experience, or brand/reputation. Your customer's discovered need for a solution is frequently the starting point for the alignment process.

3. **Footprints:** If a footprint represents the area covered by something, then your and your customer's organizational footprints refer to where your respective businesses are located, as well as how you are organized to do business. Where are your customer's

resources located? How does your customer want to buy? Are they buying locally? Nationally? Regionally? Globally? Can you align the way you sell to the way your customer buys? It sounds easy, yet it's not uncommon to see organizations of all sizes struggling with this very issue. Your inability or unwillingness to do business the way your customer wants to do business can jeopardize effective alignment.

4. **Cultures:** Cultural alignment is a powerful enabler that can sometimes help you overcome shortcomings in other areas. When organizations connect on a cultural basis, competitive disadvantages can be reduced, even if the solution itself is not as strong as others available or the footprints are not an ideal match. Strong cultural alignment can enable suppliers and customers to work together when other areas of alignment are lacking. A lack of cultural alignment can be an equally powerful disabler.

5. **Business objectives:** In B2B commerce, the strongest alignment occurs when your objectives align with your customer's in ways that enable each party to be successful. Aligning business objectives establishes a virtually unshakable foundation for value creation and co-creation and creates a fertile environment for collaboration, co-discovery, credibility, and trust—the strongest variables in the alignment equation. When you successfully align your organization's business objectives with your customer's objectives, significant competitive advantage can be the result.

Consider when you have been aligned or misaligned with your customer, and what their perception was in each of the alignment dimensions discussed above.

Internal Alignment and the Importance of Your Internal Network. The primary goal of internal alignment is ensuring that your sales or account team operates in an environment that embraces the sharing of customer information, collaboration about strategy, and the pooling of resources to ensure the strongest possible engagement with your customer—anywhere in the world. If you're not aligned internally and don't have a network of people within your organization who are committed to both your success and your customer's, it's highly likely your customer will know. But it matters, because if the customer senses your internal misalignment, they will feel uncomfortable and may believe they are being put at unnecessary risk because you and your team don't have your act together.

Based on our experience with clients, we have observed that internal misalignment typically manifests itself in four specific areas. If you can't answer each of the following questions with a resounding yes, then you should be prepared to explain why to your customer:

1. **Is your organization able to present one face to your customer?** Customers get frustrated when doing business with a single supplier feels like doing business with multiple companies, especially when they're dealing with people in different parts of a country or around the world. This happens more often than it should, and it's not surprising when you consider the challenges of doing business across regions, as well as the speed of business today. The result can be diminished credibility and trust with the customer, not to mention the risk that the customer might feel when presented with two or more versions of the truth.

2. **Are your organization's communications with your customer consistent?** When a customer asks three people in your company the same question and gets three different responses, you have a problem. This inconsistency can happen for a variety of reasons, including lack of communication within your company, no external messaging strategy, and a siloed organizational structure. Sometimes it's excusable—most times it is not. Unfortunately, when it occurs, everybody loses. Your customer wants to know that your team in the United States is saying the same thing as your teams in Germany, Brazil, and Singapore. You can't maintain a trust-based relationship if multiple people from your organization are communicating different information. The impact of this inconsistency is exacerbated when your customer's team *is* aligned

internally, because they'll realize that your team *isn't* aligned internally, and they'll talk with each other about it.

3. **Are you deploying the strengths of your team on the customer's behalf through team-to-team alignment?** To deploy your team's strengths on your customer's behalf, you must first understand how others within your organization are engaging with the customer, and for what purpose. When this deployment is working well, a powerful environment of team-to-team alignment is created. However, this doesn't just happen. The first step takes place within your own organization. To ensure the pooling of strengths, competencies, and information on behalf of the customer, the members of your internal team must be comfortable "showing their cards" by comparing notes with their colleagues. Remember, your customer can sense when individuals from your company have conflicting objectives or personal agendas.

   A client of Dave's that was seeking a sales performance improvement provider gave him very clear direction on how they wanted to engage with and learn about each of three firms being considered. Dave communicated those points to each provider's chief sales officer, only to learn later that a local salesperson from one firm was either never informed of the protocol or simply disregarded it. That provider was eliminated from further consideration. It was a significant lost opportunity for the provider, and a difficult lesson learned.

   Customer-facing professionals who align their team members' strengths with the needs of their customers create value for both parties through effective team-to-team alignment.

4. **Can you leverage the value of your entire organization on behalf of the customer?** Customers want to work with sales professionals who can *deliver the organization*, which means they want to work with people who can help them access your company's most valuable resources. Customers often express significant frustration with navigating their suppliers' organizations, especially

when their time has been wasted and redundancies occur. On the other hand, when your customer believes that their key contact is a conduit to resources critical to their own success, confidence and comfort develops. This typically translates into enhanced credibility and greater trust in the salesperson, the account manager, or the customer service professional with whom your customer is most closely aligned.

Whether a customer is connecting with your company's salespeople, account managers, service personnel, accounts receivable team, legal team, or executives, you must be certain that your internal customer-facing team is aligned. Internal departmental differences tend to fade when an important client succeeds, making it even easier for colleagues to align.

You can effectively connect with your customer's team only when you're fully confident that your internal alignment is where it should be, however you get there.

External Alignment and the Importance of Your Customer Network.

The primary goal of external alignment is to build a deep and wide network of sponsors and supporters throughout your customer's organization. Something very special happens when you connect and integrate resources with your customer's team and build relationships based on trust, credibility, and value creation. And because there isn't enough time for customers to sponsor and support all of their suppliers, they focus on the ones they consider to be most important.

So how do customers determine which suppliers are most important? They can tell who's invested the time to get to know their company. If you've explored possibilities together, helped them build a vision of their success, elevated the conversation, and demonstrated actionable awareness about their external drivers, business objectives, and internal challenges, then you've established credibility, a commitment to value creation, and a trust-based relationship. When these elements converge, you and your customer have developed something special. In any given opportunity, the odds are good that only one provider among many will fully accomplish this.

Your sponsors and supporters are the people in your customer's organization who favor you and want you to win. If you've effectively aligned with them, they may even have come to care about your personal success as well as that of your organization, which is a strong position to find yourself in when you are competing for business.

Of course, it's unlikely that you are the only supplier pursuing an opportunity. Your competitors will have sponsors and supporters who favor them. As you analyze your customer's decision team, it's important to recognize where each individual member stands in terms of preference, and then compare each one's relative political strengths. When RFPs are issued, the customer usually promises impartiality, but the reality is that influencers, recommenders, and decision-team members typically have their own predispositions. Sometimes we're asked, "What about people who say they have no preference for one supplier or another?" In our experience, few people are truly neutral when it's time to make a decision to buy. This can be a significant advantage or disadvantage. After several decades of analyzing wins and losses, we firmly believe that no single factor is more important to winning an opportunity than the presence of an executive sponsor on the customer's decision team.

When you have customer sponsorship and strong support at all levels of your customer's organization, the advantage is yours and your likelihood of winning increases dramatically.

The Importance of Aligning at Multiple Levels. Think about your last RFP. It outlined your customer's needs in exhaustive detail, but did it tell you anything about personal wants as expressed by individual members of the customer's team? Probably not. People are rarely comfortable documenting their personal desires and preferences in a business environment, and an RFP is not the place for it anyway. Yet those wants almost always exist, and their existence influences how decisions get made. The problem is, as soon as the RFP goes out (packed full with professional needs and organizational requirements), the conversation tends to shut down. At that point, it's too late to sit with a decision team member and ask, "Why does this matter to *you*?" "What's the main thing that you are focused on in this evaluation?" or "If it's close between two respondents, what will break the tie?" You won't find those answers in the RFP.

In Strategy 5, we explored the faulty logic behind the traditional notion that calling too low in your customer organization is a complete waste of time and effort. Again, giving your attention only to decision makers and approvers may seem logical on its face, but the inherent flaws become more apparent during alignment, and can even be fatal in today's buying environment. Why should the wants and needs of a middle manager matter to you? Because the executive who doesn't have the time or expertise to gather and understand complex details of the decision criteria typically asks management or an individual contributor/SME to explain them. When this occurs, the work you've done to build a network within your customer's organization pays off.

As referenced in Strategy 5 and illustrated by Figure 6-1, an individual's function and role at every level of your customer's organization shapes his or her perspective. Senior executives typically focus on how the company is doing. Middle managers tend to think more about the success of their

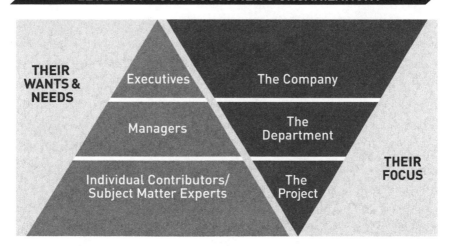

HOW SHOULD YOU ALIGN WITH DIFFERENT LEVELS OF YOUR CUSTOMER'S ORGANIZATION?

THEIR WANTS & NEEDS

Executives — The Company

Managers — The Department

Individual Contributors/ Subject Matter Experts — The Project

THEIR FOCUS

Figure 6-1. **How should you align with different levels of your customer's organization?**

business unit or department. Individual contributors and SMEs tend to be concerned with their specific project or personal performance. These considerations all matter, and the more you know about what's important to key individuals at each level, the more effectively you will connect through team-to-team alignment.

A word of caution: If you're looking to be in relationship with your customer for the long haul, stepping on and stepping over people at lower and middle levels as you claw your way to the top is not an effective strategy. People remember, and they get promoted. As a sales professional, your responsibility is to identify who can influence the decision and understand what's important to them, both professionally and personally. You need to know what's in it for each individual. This involves an investment of time, but if you don't do it before the RFP comes out, it'll be too late. You'll have only what your competitors have—plenty of data and information, but little insight and actionable awareness. You'll fall victim to your own lack of alignment with the customer.

Alignment Is As Valuable to Your Customer As It Is to You

Alignment requires a time investment from both you and your customer, but it's well worth the effort. With effective alignment, your customer gains access to your organization's resources and solutions, empowering them to meet their internal challenges and business objectives. Alignment also makes navigating your organization easier and provides your customer with consistency, predictability, and timely access. Effective alignment enables customers to make things happen in less time and with fewer steps.

Your vantage point is much the same. You want access to the right customer contacts, along with the insight and actionable awareness that each can provide. When you have a great relationship in middle management, you can sometimes gain access to the executive level by asking for an introduction. If your alignment has been effective, and you've developed an authentic, trust-based relationship, your customer will likely oblige. The broader your network of customer sponsors and supporters, the more opportunities you will have to expand it.

Gerhard Gschwandtner, founder and publisher of *Selling Power* magazine, offers this insight about the significance of alignment in today's selling environment:

> "Alignment is a little like buttoning your shirt. When the first button is wrong, all the others will be wrong as well. Alignment is what happens in sales when the salesperson makes the connections with the customer that result in deeper insights into their problems, buying process, and decision teams. Time and time again sales outcomes are determined by how much the salesperson really understood about these three things."

Potential Points of Alignment. Strong alignment paves the way for effective positioning. Without it, many of your words, presentations, and sales strategies will fall on deaf ears. Let's dig deeper into the four most likely points for effective customer alignment, and consider where to make these potentially high-impact customer connections:

1. **Defining your customer's decision criteria, decision process, and decision team.** There's typically an opportunity to align with what your customer will deem most important in making their decision. There's also an opportunity to align with how they plan to make their decision. But you can't align effectively unless you know who you will be engaging with throughout the customer's decision process. In numerous opportunities we've observed, the winning supplier was able to achieve significant levels of alignment in each of these three areas. In every case, that alignment began with a discovery effort that brought about the understanding and actionable awareness to move forward effectively and with confidence.

2. **Assembling and aligning your sales/account team with your customer's decision team.** Team-to-team alignment makes each person a potential connection point. When you achieve a stronger level of alignment than your competitors, a winning sale is

usually not far away. If alignment were easy, then every provider would do it. It isn't, so relatively few even try.

Before you can align teams with the customer, you must first define the roles of your sales and account team members. It sounds straightforward, but it can be complicated by such issues as customer/account ownership, control of the sale, and regional differences in sales approach, among others. Your customer is primarily concerned with the value that each member of your customer-facing team brings to the relationship. A sales/account team with clarity about each member's role, responsibility, and value to the customer's team becomes significantly empowered to align and engage effectively.

3. **Assessing your customer's requirements for a potential fit with your solutions.** This point of alignment is about determining the potential fit between your customer's requirements and challenges and your solutions. In some cases, the assessment reveals a strong fit, so the decision to proceed is reasonably clear. In other cases, the alignment between your solution and your customer's requirements is not as strong as you would like it to be. When this occurs, you have a decision to make. Since the fit won't be any better after the sale than it was before, the question becomes, "What's worth more—the short-term sale or the long-term customer relationship?" Every supplier has to judge wisely about when to proceed and when to step back. Remember, effective discovery and alignment gives you the insight and actionable awareness to make the right decision.

4. **Finalizing your customer's drivers, objectives, and challenges.** In Strategy 5, we discussed elevating the dialogue by focusing on your customer's external drivers and pressures, business objectives, internal challenges, and personal success criteria. You don't have to align with every driver, objective, and challenge that your customer has, but you do have to align with enough of them to position your solutions and differentiate your unique value in a way that sets you apart from your competitors.

As your customer's business conditions and requirements evolve throughout the opportunity, it's inevitable that you'll need to update and build on what you learned in your early discovery. When you engage effectively and help your customer validate their drivers, objectives, and challenges, you can further elevate your conversation with the customer and find yourself connected to and aligned with the changing reality and dynamics of their business.

Bringing it all together, you'll find that effective alignment can dramatically change the direction of the sale. The salesperson with the most thorough understanding of what is most important to the customer has insight and actionable awareness that others do not. But it's the customer conversations and engagement process—the questions you ask, the innovations you suggest, and the best practices that you deploy—that make it clear that you engage differently. Understanding how your customer views you and your organization can be powerful, so let's look at how successful customer-facing teams assess their relationships with their most important customers.

Assessing Customer Relationships. Evaluating customer relationships in a hierarchal manner is not a new concept, but unless you are a SAMA community member, you may be unfamiliar with the following approach to assessment, which is predicated upon specific definitions and gleaned from observed customer responses.

Working with SAMA and the SAMA community, Steve and PMI formalized a customer relationship assessment tool to provide simple analytics that describe the primary characteristics of the four relationship levels most prevalent in modern customer engagement: *vendor, preferred supplier, planning partner*, and *trusted advisor*. Customers evaluate their relationships with suppliers at these levels, which can be described by a proven and consistent set of criteria. This tool can assist you in understanding not only how the customer views their relationship with your organization, their relationship with you, and in a new business situation, their relationship with your competitor—the incumbent.

When assessing customer relationships, some salespeople and account managers tend to be optimistic. It's not unusual to hear one claim, after working with a customer, that their relationship is strong, at both the professional and personal levels. We all want to think that our customers like and appreciate us, and this type of positive thinking is easy to understand. But can being overly optimistic and unrealistic about how the customer feels be hazardous to your sales health? Absolutely. It happens every day.

As we explore the four levels, think about your own relationships. Consider how one of your most important customers perceives your company and their relationship with you in light of the characteristics expressed at each level.

1. **Vendor.** When you're a vendor, everything tends to be competitive and your customer may have no better reason for doing business with you than convenience, which usually means you're simply the low-price provider. They buy from you because you are the cheapest or easiest to contract with, not because you solve problems or create customer value. If this conjures up the word "commodity" in your mind, it's for good reason; most commodity providers live here. At the vendor level, you have lots of competition and the customer has little, if any, loyalty to you. You can drive a lot of business as a vendor, but you typically have to work harder for it and endure higher stress levels while doing so.

2. **Preferred supplier.** At the preferred supplier level, closed doors begin to open, and your customer becomes more interested in your planning efforts on their behalf. Having invested the time in discovering what's important to your customer, you're able to articulate what you know in a way that builds credibility. Your customer recognizes and acknowledges your solutions, as well as the positive impact that these solutions have had on their business. The relationship has grown, and now includes supporters within the customer organization who help you understand what's happening. *Convenience* has evolved into *importance* and the customer prefers you over most other providers.

3. **Planning partner.** Something profound happens in the evolution from preferred supplier to planning partner—you graduate

from being *important* to being *necessary* to your customer's business. Indicating a substantive shift in your customer's perspective on your company, this jump is not accidental. You've invested a significant amount of time and resources into the relationship, and your customer sees you as a partner with whom they can plan and consult. Your customer also has clear ideas about what sets your company apart from others and an understanding of your value and value proposition for them. At this level, based on the existence of strong supporters and perhaps even a sponsor or two, your company may even be engaging in noncompetitive opportunities.

Certainly, planning partner status is a great place to be in a customer relationship, and in some cases, may be as good as it gets. But in those rare instances where trust is strong, past proven value is abundant, and collaboration and value creation and co-creation are the order of the day, you've earned the right to be more. From planning partner, you ascend to a position that is typically available to only one organization in a market for any given customer—trusted advisor.

4. **Trusted advisor.** As a trusted advisor, you are at the essence of the customer's business. *Essence* is a carefully chosen word, inspired by an experience that Steve had with a client. While interviewing one of the client's strategic accounts, Steve found himself speaking with the head of global procurement about her perspective on the connection between the two organizations. She described the relationship as one that was *critical* to her business. She was emphatic that, as a result of years of strong performance and value creation, she wanted this supplier in particular to be successful because she believed they were *essential* to her company's growth. Is it easy to build this type of relationship with strategic sourcing and procurement professionals? Perhaps not, but it can be done, and when it is, you find yourself in very exclusive company!

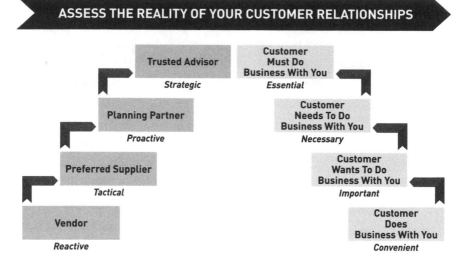

Figure 6-2. Assess the reality of your customer relationships.

Wherever there is a customer/supplier relationship that can be described with words like *important, necessary, essential, partner,* or *advisor* (Figure 6-2), you can bet you'll find strong alignment between the parties, with sponsors and supporters in the room when the organizations get together.

Testing the Effectiveness of Your Alignment

The following six sets of questions will help you determine your level of alignment with your customer:

1. **Do you understand what's important to each member of your customer's decision team?** What are those things? If not, why don't you know?

2. **Have you connected the members of your sales/account team with your customer's decision team?** Who are you connected with? If not, when do you intend to do so, and how do you intend to do it?

3. **Have you established credibility and built trust-based relationships with your customer's decision team members?** With whom? What do they believe that you and your organization will do to help ensure their success?

4. **Do you have strong support at all levels of your customer's decision team?** Why do these team members care? What do they believe that you and your organization will do to help ensure their success that others will not?

5. **Have you developed executive-level sponsor(s) for this opportunity?** How about at the management and individual contributor levels? Why do these executives, managers, and individual contributors care? From their perspectives, what makes you different from your competitors?

6. **Have you validated your customer's drivers, objectives, and challenges relative to this opportunity?** Have they changed and, if so, why? Is it becoming clear how to align your solutions and value with what your customer values most?

Position the Fit: Competing for Customer Mindshare

IN SECTION I, you learned how to research your customer and elevate the conversation, focusing largely on possibilities and building a vision of success. In this section, through your discovery, you've gained a thorough understanding of the external drivers, business objectives, and internal challenges that are impacting your customer. And through your alignment, you've connected your company's resources to your customer's team and worked to establish trust and credibility, paving the way for creating and co-creating value.

With positioning, the battle for *customer mindshare* begins. It's going to be a struggle, because you and your competitors all want the same thing: to maximize the amount of space that you occupy in your customer's thoughts and awareness. Capturing the largest possible "share of mind" or awareness won't happen unless you give your customer valid reasons to think of you in the context of whatever is happening in their world. Effective positioning is precisely how you do it.

Over the years, we've heard more than a few salespeople and account managers imply that when an RFP arrives, it's a good day. That's certainly one way to look at it. Unfortunately, many suppliers fail to realize that they are starting from behind in the fight for customer mindshare, even with an RFP in hand. If you haven't been asked for your insights in advance of a formal request being issued, and your input is nowhere to be found when you read it, it's probably because a competitor got there first. Just as unsettling, that competitor has gained additional advantage, because while you weren't increasing your share of mind, they were increasing theirs.

In the positioning phase of *Engage/Win/Grow*, the fight is on, and you've got to be in it to win it.

Positioning Is All About the Fit

In the battle for customer mindshare, the playing field is crowded and the competition is fierce. If you don't sense a battle raging, it's not because there isn't one; it's because you're not in the fight. Even so, your company is already being positioned, counter-positioned, or poorly positioned in the customer's mind. If you don't want to be misunderstood or left out altogether, the onus rests squarely on you to be proactive in guiding your customer's awareness of how your offerings line up with their needs and objectives. In other words, it's how you choose to position your fit with your customer's business.

We define *positioning* as developing or building customer mindshare by creating a positive perception of your solutions, advantages, and business value. It's ensuring that your customer understands how your product or service is the best solution for their needs and offers the most value for their organization. It's all about the fit.

The concept of *fit* is simple, but its application can be complex. Fit occurs when your customer says, "I get it. This makes sense to me. It aligns with the way we see moving forward." What that customer really means is, "I've got choices, but based on how you explained [positioned] what your company can provide, I believe you are my best option, or among my best options."

Digging a little deeper into our definition of positioning, there is intentional significance for using the terms *developing* and *building*. Both words indicate proactivity—positioning doesn't happen by itself; you must cause it to happen. If you don't, you risk empowering a skilled competitor to counter-position, or worse, develop negative customer mindshare about your company.

It's incumbent on you as a salesperson or account manager to develop positive mindshare with your customer, and to do it early. Take charge of creating a positive perception—don't let another supplier take control, don't rely on market forces, and certainly don't allow customers to (mis)understand your company through hearsay or innuendo. Your goal is to articulate clearly who you are and how you solve problems, bring advantages, and deliver unique value to your customer.

Let's focus for just a moment on *unique value*. Most suppliers can claim value of some sort or another, but can they articulate what distinguishes their product or service from yours? Can you? These are important considerations, because if you can identify and express your uniqueness, and help the customer perceive that your uniqueness fits into their needs in a way that no one else's does, then mindshare starts to swing in your direction.

To Position or Be Positioned? That Is the Question

Positioning happens, one way or another, every time you connect with your customer. When you position your strengths effectively, your competitive advantage can linger long after the sale has ended.

A client of Steve's once told him, "I do my best selling when my customer is *not* buying, so that when they *are* buying, I'm up where the air is clear and clean." Taking a literal approach to elevating the conversation through positioning, he also understood that positioning is not a standalone, one-time event, or even a series of isolated or disconnected activities. Positioning is an ongoing process.

Before the sale, for example, when you were exploring possibilities and envisioning success with your customer, you were (in effect) positioning your company as distinct from competing organizations by engaging differently. It's very possible, even likely, that no one else was having that conversation or engaging the customer in the same way.

Today's customers almost universally express a desire to have fewer rather than more suppliers in any given space, yet most RFP environments involve anywhere from three to five participants. So, based purely on percentages, your likelihood of winning falls somewhere between 20 and 33 percent. Taken a step further, those percentages become dramatically lower if you have not had some level of input and impact on the RFP. Positioning is designed to improve those odds, and it works.

Is your customer's perception always accurate? Of course not. It's entirely possible to become poorly positioned because members of your customer's team may not be clear about their own requirements, your company's fit with these requirements, or both. Your job as a professional and an expert in the *Engage/Win/Grow* approach is to make sure that misunderstanding doesn't happen, and that your customer's perception is grounded in reality.

Start with Your Customer, Not with Your Product

Anyone who's been around the sales business for more than a few years is probably familiar with a selling technique that goes something like this: The salesperson describes a product's features, extols its benefits to the customer, asks a pointed question designed to elicit, solicit, or extract a positive response . . . and then waits. No matter how long it takes for a response, no matter how awkward or uncomfortable, the silence stretches on until the customer speaks.

That's not positioning. It's the seller's attempt to paint the customer into a corner with only one good escape—expressing agreement. It's pushing the customer around. That may have worked decades ago, but it won't work now. Positioning, on the other hand, begins with thinking about your customer and never stops putting your customer first. No awkward silence is required.

When you're in front of your customer, you have to make it count. You have to be in the battle for customer mindshare. You have to establish that your company, your product, your solutions, your value, and you are your customer's best fit.

Earning the Right to Position. What does success look like to your customer? There is no better way to understand than to ask. Yet customers frequently tell us that this is a question no salesperson ever raises. We hear them say that their reps like to talk about the RFP and its requirements.

And that salespeople tend to focus more on the formal statement of need than on what's behind it. But our experience is that salespeople rarely ask about their customer's vision of success. So consider this: if everyone wants to be successful, why wouldn't you want to give your customer a chance to talk about it? Understanding your customer's vision of success is just one example of how you earn the right to position.

You earn the right to position through discovery. As we discussed in Strategy 5, discovery is all about understanding your customer's business. You achieve that understanding by asking value-focused questions, which provide insights into your customer's external drivers, business objectives, internal challenges, and success criteria. But there's more to discovery than a simple transmission of knowledge and data from one party to another.

If you have been effective at discovering what's going on in your customer's world, and you let your customer know through the questions you have asked, then something important has happened. Credibility has been established. You cared enough to ask. You were astute enough to listen. You were professional enough to hear what your customer really said. Maybe you even surmised a few things that your customer didn't actually say.

Remember, when you're doing your discovery, you're not waiting to talk. You're listening. You're hearing. You're interpreting. And it doesn't hurt to take copious notes. Even if you have a photographic memory and can recall everything with perfect accuracy, your customer should see you taking down what they are telling you. They should experience you doing your discovery. They should see you listen.

Effective discovery elevates the dialogue. By demonstrating that you understand what's important to your customer, you rise even further above the noise level to where you want to be—where the airspace is clear, clean, and much less crowded.

You also earn the right to position through alignment. As we discussed in Strategy 6, alignment allows you to connect and integrate your resources with the members of your customer's team. As with discovery, more happens here than just a transfer of information. Being effective at aligning with your customer means making powerful connections. It means your relationship is far greater than a casual acquaintance, and goes much deeper than, for example, a LinkedIn connection that is accepted and then neglected. If your alignment efforts have been effective, you have developed a relationship built on trust, credibility, and value creation.

Asking generic questions such as, "What keeps you up at night?" or making requests like, "Tell me about your business," demonstrates that you have not gone the distance in your discovery and alignment. These types of queries and requests have little or no place in the contemporary selling environment. They expose you as a vendor. They reveal that you have not earned the right to position. They cause you to sound like everyone else. They demonstrate that you have not established trust and credibility.

By putting discovery and alignment to work, you can position yourself more effectively, and in a broader fashion, because you've made the effort. You've invested the time. You've earned the right. Your customer is going to speak with you much differently and with a different voice than they will use with vendors because they know you understand what's truly important to them. You've earned the right to position.

Effective discovery and alignment help you capture customer mindshare.

Positioning Up and Down the Organization. When your authors were trained to sell, we were told to spend our time with the people who can make the decision to buy, which meant people in senior positions. But neither of us has ever believed that we need relationships only with those at the top and, as it turns out, we are right. You need to develop sponsors and supporters at all levels of your customer's organization and, just as importantly, you don't want enemies or antagonists at any level.

You must position differently depending on the level of the person you engage with, because someone at the senior executive level has different wants and needs than the middle manager or an individual contributor (see Figure 6-1). Through effective discovery and alignment, you build the foundation for successful positioning.

We've already established that every contact with your customer represents a positioning opportunity. There are, however, particular types of activities that are prime for positioning:

- **Assessing customer requirements for potential fit with your solutions.** An assessment of how well your solutions fit with your customer's requirements involves some level of interaction. This interaction is fertile ground, both for understanding the relative strengths and weaknesses of your fit and for developing opportunities for positioning. Think of it this way: If competitors are pressuring the customer to agree that they offer the best of everything, while your approach is to first understand how to meet the customer's requirements, you're already well-positioned before you ever discuss your offerings.

- **Finalizing your customer's external drivers, business objectives, and internal challenges as they relate to the opportunity.** The benefit here is twofold—you get to find out what's important to position and align with, and you create an opportunity to ask questions such as, "Can you prioritize these drivers for me?" "Would you give me a timeline for these objectives?" "What will success look like for this initiative or project one year from now?" Some of your most effective positioning, especially early on, is accomplished here. Even better, you just may be the only one asking these types of questions.

- **Verifying who your competitors are, and their perceived strengths and weaknesses.** Some customers are very open about this; others are decidedly not. Through this verification, you'll gain insights and information that will help you. Opening a discussion about your competitors may be inappropriate and perceived negatively in some places sometimes, depending on your customer's business culture, but suffice it to say, if you can get this information tactfully, you should.

- **Developing a customer-specific value proposition for this opportunity.** In selling today, there should be a customer-specific value proposition for each and every sale. This need not be a global, marketing-driven, high-level deal promotion, but rather one that is based precisely on the external drivers, business objectives, and internal challenges affecting that specific and unique customer. It should clearly connect your solutions and value to your customer's internal challenges and business objectives.

- **Positioning your solution advantages with your customer's decision team.** Even the most highly cohesive decision team is composed of individuals who have their own respective wants, needs, and priorities. You can address these by engaging with each team member and positioning your solution advantages in alignment with what is most important to each of them. You will already know what is most important to individual team members because of your discovery, and you will have achieved some level of alignment with them as part of the process.

- **Building a network of customer sponsors and supporters that favor you.** During debriefing, when the reasons behind wins and losses are being assessed, success or failure can almost always be attributed, at least in part, to the influence of sponsors and supporters. We've discussed sponsors and supporters in earlier strategies, but because sponsors and supporters are so important, it's worth taking a closer look at who they are.

   A supporter can be defined simply as a representative from your customer's organization who wants you to win. A sponsor, on the other hand, is a supporter who is willing to assume some level of risk for you and your company. What does that mean? Sponsors will coach you on how to win, or will stand up and be heard on your behalf. They might say, "There's a reason we favor this supplier, even if they're not the cheapest," or "There's a reason why we've done business with this company for the last five years, even though they may not have everything we want."

   You can do some very effective positioning through a network of sponsors and supporters.

- **Confirming the fit of your solution with key members of the customer's decision team.** When your customer's decision team is populated with supporters and sponsors, you have the ability to confirm how your solution fits their needs. You can discuss what you bring to the table. You can suggest why you think your fit is superior. You can seek their agreement, or invite their disagreement.

Early-Stage Versus Later-Stage Positioning. Your customer's readiness to receive certain types of information depends on where they are in their buying process. If you try to position specifics, such as detailed wants and needs, before your customer is ready and willing to listen and hear what you have to say, then your positioning falls on deaf ears and you fail to acquire mindshare. You can even backslide and lose mindshare because your customer feels uncomfortable with your timing.

Early-stage positioning tends to occur at a very high level. You are not going to walk into a room with the customer's team members early in the opportunity and get specific about things that they may not yet be ready to talk to you about. Early stage positioning is more general. You're trying to build credibility. You can offer help, but keep it less prescriptive. You won't necessarily connect to the specific wants and needs of the customer's team members with early positioning, but it could be a good time to discuss evolving market trends or what you've done for others in their industry.

Later-stage positioning is more focused and much more directed to the level of each individual. Is she a senior executive? Is he the manager of a business unit? An individual contributor or SME? As your customer moves through their buying process and you become more aligned with them, you can leverage your credibility to build trust-based relationships and connect with their specific wants and needs, especially as they relate to the individual. This is where you selectively position your strengths and, in the process of doing so, help the customer's team members understand how you and your organization can help them meet their objectives.

Early-stage positioning basically sets the table for later-stage positioning, and it's based on your effective discovery and alignment.

What Is Being Positioned?

All too frequently, suppliers approach customers with a broad portfolio of solutions, and their salespeople and account managers assume that the customer knows how it fits their own business. Let's be very clear. You're battling for mindshare. It's a crowded space. The customer is bombarded with an excess of information every single day. You simply cannot expect them to make those connections themselves. And if you don't do it for them, the customer is likely to think that you can't, or you won't, or worse, that you don't really understand those connections yourself.

Geoffrey James, Contributing Editor at *Inc.* magazine, and an expert in the area of what is and isn't working in sales today, offers this perspective:

> "Some salespeople get off to a solid start, gaining knowledge and building relationships they didn't have, only to find themselves counter-positioned, out-positioned, mis-positioned, or not positioned at all because they failed to have a deliberate strategy for entering the mind of the customer. Then, when they realize they are where they are, it's too late because someone else is now occupying that space."

It's up to you to make connections through proactive positioning, and in situations where you have effectively completed your discovery and alignment, it becomes more than possible. It's the natural next step.

As Figure 7-1 shows, the following components can help you position effectively by taking your offering in the broadest terms and deconstructing it into six parts:

1. **Products:** *the configurations of your company's offerings that solve your customer's problems.* These are the things you offer to your markets.

2. **Resources:** *the people, partners, technology, and infrastructure that you provide to your customers.* This is who and what you bring to the customer relationship to make things happen.

3. **Expertise:** *the knowledge and skills that you apply and transfer to your customer.* From time to time, we've been asked whether a resource and an expert are the same. They absolutely are not. Resources are many, but expertise is rare. When you have expert knowledge that you can transfer to your customer in the form of best practices to help their business improve, it's very powerful and very valuable. Also, most of us have observed (and, ideally, participated in) the significant movement toward leveraging thought leadership through social selling to attract, influence, and nurture customers. Isn't that all about expertise?

4. **Services:** *the value-added services that solve your customer's problems and create value.* What are you going to do after the sale? How will you collaborate with your customer? As you're servicing the account, how do you solve problems? How do you create value? What makes it a value-added service rather than something expected that everyone offers? As one customer said, "Services are the seller's commitment to make promises come true."

5. **Customer experience:** *the experience that your company has had with other organizations that are comparable to this customer.* This can include experiences in your customer's industry, market, region, or any area where the customer might find comfort in the idea that their risk is reduced because you have been there before and done that. Other customers and stories about past successes can be part of your solution. That's the reason testimonials and case studies, when used properly, are so powerful.

6. **Brand and reputation:** *your company's reputation, corporate image, and proven track record of success that provide assurance to your customer. Brand* and *reputation* may be similar, but there's a distinction to be made between these two terms. Here's an example of how we see the differences: The first time you buy a consumer product, such as a car, you might make the purchase based

on brand, or you might at least be drawn into the showroom or onto the lot because of what you know about the brand. When you buy a second car from the same manufacturer, you do it because the brand has earned a reputation with you personally. In B2B engagement, especially with two organizations that have a long history of doing business together, we're talking less about brand and more about the reputation that your company has developed with the customer. It's about your track record with your customer, and what you have done to provide assurance, to create value, and to reduce their risk.

Thinking about how competitors will position themselves to your customer can provide perspective and prompt considerations that effectively shape and impact the type of competitive strategy you build and deploy. And even if you don't like to do it, you're better off thinking like the competition and anticipating their positioning strategy than not. Do you have a stronger portfolio of potential value, or does the competition? It's something to consider.

THE CORE COMPONENTS OF POSITIONING

Products	The configurations of your offerings that solve customer problems
Resources	The people, partners, technology, infrastructure that you provide to your customers
Expertise	The knowledge and skills that you apply and transfer to your customers
Services	Your value-added services that solve customer problems and create value
Customer Experience	Your experience with comparable customer organizations
Brand/Reputation	Your reputation, corporate image, and proven track record of success that provide assurance to the customer

Figure 7-1. The core components of positioning.

Planning to Win: The Intersection of Alignment and Positioning

Dave once heard a client say, "If we get alignment and positioning right, we'll win every opportunity." While we can't fully agree (as you will see in Strategy 8, differentiation requires some additional work), the point is clear. If you have done effective discovery, established credibility, built a trust-based relationship through alignment, and put strong positioning into place, you've distanced yourself from the competition. Figure 7-2 provides a visual for evaluating your progress.

In a new opportunity, you may start out with very little alignment and positioning. This is typically the case in a new account, or when you are selling into a new area of an existing customer's business where you don't have established relationships. In these situations, your course is clear. When you're planning to win, you'll need to *invest* time and resources to be successful.

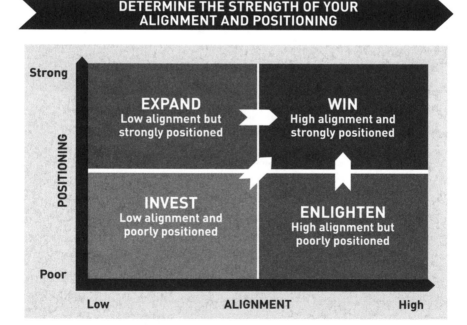

Figure 7-2. Determine the strength of your alignment and positioning.

Sometimes your alignment is relatively strong, but you are proposing something in an area of your customer's business where you don't have a track record—you haven't worked with this business unit, division, or department before, or it's a brand new customer. In these scenarios, you leverage your alignment to find ways to *enlighten* the customer about the type of solutions and value that you and your company can offer. This is where your trust-based relationships and past proven value in other areas of your customer's business, or other comparable customers' businesses, can work strongly in your favor.

On the other hand, sometimes you and your customer have a history together and you are well positioned for additional business, but the opportunity involves a division or decision team with whom you have never worked. In these situations, it's time to *expand* your customer relationships to include these individuals and begin to build credibility and trust with them, as you have with others in their organization. Again, look to your history with your customer to open doors for you that may have otherwise been closed.

Note that in all of these cases, the objective is to move you and your organization "up and to the right" with the strength of your alignment and positioning. As you do so, you increase the likelihood that you and your sales/account team will *win* the business. Unless your price is unrealistic based on your customer's expectations, or a competitor is even better aligned and positioned than you are, it's hard to lose when your alignment and positioning are the strongest among your peers. Consider this: You've essentially completed your discovery and alignment, and you're ready to move forward equipped with fresh insight and trust-based relationships. When you launch your positioning efforts, think about what you are trying to accomplish. Do you have a specific positioning strategy in mind? We believe the following strategy types are among the most likely to be effective. Whichever you choose, you can expect to have to modify and evolve your strategy as the opportunity advances.

- **Raise the dialogue:** Elevate the level of the discussion, and get to your customer's executive level. This process begins before the sale and never stops.

- **Solve the problem:** Develop a solution that your customer believes will solve their business problem and enable their success.

- **Prove the value:** Confirm your solution fit and validate your value proposition with your customer.

- **Change the landscape:** Provide reasons that your customer should change their evaluation criteria and selection approach.

- **Expand the vision:** Increase and extend your customer's vision of a solution to pursue a larger sale.

- **Divide the opportunity:** Compete for only a portion of the business because your fit is stronger and the likelihood of winning is greater.

- **Develop the proposal:** Build a winning proposal that exceeds customer requirements and demonstrates your organization's commitment to your customer's success.

- **Provide references:** Reduce your customer's sense of risk by providing examples of where and how you've delivered comparable value to other customers in similar situations.

When you think about planning to win, what you're really doing is mapping these and other pieces together, in the right sequence, to happen at the right times. When you engage, win, and grow, it becomes natural. Your customer is ready to hear what you have to say and will respond, not because you tried to control or manipulate them, but because they see potential value.

Planning to win involves elements of both science and art. The science is about making the right moves based on what has proven to be effective in the past. Think of this as leveraging predictable, repeatable best practices to drive future sales performance. The art is in choosing the right positioning strategy and executing it based on the insight gained through discovery and alignment.

One caution before we end this chapter: salespeople and account managers have been known to believe that their customer is buying on price, and that price is the only consideration. Yet, when we talk to customers after the sale, we rarely hear this. We recognize that procurement departments send up flares indicating that it's all about price and delivery. We get that—it's the role they must play. But when you talk to people in business, it is extremely rare to hear that any decision has been made purely on price. When you're not the cheapest and the outcome isn't what you want, you may feel better believing that you never had a chance, because it was "all about price." But ask yourself this question: If you knew this, and you knew that you were not the low-price provider, then why did you choose to stay in and compete?

Sometimes you stay because it takes courage to pull out, especially in difficult selling environments. We're not suggesting that you remove yourself from the opportunity when the going gets tough, but rather that you build a strong customer-specific value proposition that allows you to differentiate effectively so that your customer's decision to award their business to you is the most logical conclusion.

That's where we're going in Strategy 8—how do you finalize and win the business through effective differentiation? The next move is yours; it's time to capture customer preference.

Testing the Effectiveness of Your Positioning

The following six sets of questions will help you evaluate the effectiveness of your positioning with your customer:

1. **Does your customer perceive that your solution provides a strong fit for their needs and requirements?** You probably won't win if they don't. How do you know this? Who on the customer's team is telling you?

2. **Do you have, or can you develop, competitive advantage within this opportunity?** If so, how will you know? Where is that competitive advantage? Will your customer see it? Will they acknowledge it? Will they value it?

3. **Does your customer have a vision of a solution, and does that vision include you?** How do you know? Are you getting direct feedback through ongoing customer collaboration during the sales process? How has your initial vision evolved into a more focused customer-specific solution?

4. **Do you have resources available that will enable you and your organization to meet your customer's requirements and exceed their expectations?** This cannot be simply words on paper. If you sell business that you can't deliver, your success will be short term, and it will probably be the last time you engage with that customer.

5. **Have you developed an effective proposal that will solve your customer's business problems and deliver real value?** If so, what is that proposal? What are its strengths and where are its weaknesses? Will your proposal meet and exceed the customer's corporate or department investment policies?

6. **Does your customer recognize your solution and business value beyond product features and pricing?** If not now, then when will they? Are you fully prepared to differentiate yourself from your competition and win this business, and precisely how will you accomplish this?

STRATEGY 8

Differentiate the Value: Creating a Customer Preference

WE'VE COVERED QUITE A LOT of ground in Section II, and if you've been following along with a specific customer in mind, you may be feeling pretty good about where your relationship currently stands. You've conducted effective discovery and now have more than just insights: you have actionable awareness about your customer's external drivers, business objectives, and internal challenges. You've aligned and integrated your resources with your customer's team and worked to build relationships based on trust, credibility, and value creation and co-creation. And, through positioning, you've gained customer mindshare; created a positive perception of the solutions, advantages, and business value you offer; and shown your customer how your solution fits their business and addresses their challenges.

Planning to win has brought you to this point. The time has come to put your stakes in the ground and achieve competitive advantage. *Differentiation*—the process of achieving competitive advantage by creating a customer preference for the fit of your solutions and the uniqueness of your business value—makes that happen.

Making Your Plan to Win a Reality

The purpose of differentiation is to achieve competitive advantage. As a supplier, you do this by *creating a preference* for the fit of your solutions, for the uniqueness of your business value, and for a partnership with your organization. Now we're going to take a close look at how to differentiate the unique value of your offerings and create that preference. You've earned the right to differentiate through your effective discovery, alignment, and positioning. It's time to win.

To differentiate yourself and your organization effectively, you need to begin with a focus on the relationships you've built with your customer's team. Take note of the word *team* here, because in today's buying environment, there's almost always more than one buyer in the customer's organization, even for relatively small sales. As opportunities become increasingly complex, a greater number of people are likely to be involved in decision making, each bringing a personal perspective, agenda, needs, and expertise to the table. Consequently, you can count on having to differentiate yourself and your organization many times throughout your customer's buying process, and doing so at different levels.

Differentiation involves three fundamental areas where you want to create customer preference:

1. **Your solution's fit against your customer's requirements.** A strong fit in the solution area is ideal, although there are countless examples of offering arguably the best product or service and still not winning the customer's business. Clearly, the stronger your fit, the more powerful your differentiation can be. But keep this in mind: determining fit has both subjective and objective components. Effective alignment and positioning creates a platform from which you can more successfully demonstrate the overall fit of your solution against what's important to your customer (your products, resources, expertise, services, etc.).

2. **The uniqueness of your business value.** Many suppliers offer solutions, products, and services, but from the perspectives of their

customers, too few deliver true, unique business value. The concept of business value extends far beyond your products, services, and solutions; it should connect directly with your customer's external drivers, business objectives, and internal challenges. When it does, if your value is unique, you may be the only provider that can clearly demonstrate how you will ensure your customer's success by helping them meet and exceed their objectives.

3. **A partnership with your organization.** All things being equal, your goal is to be the company that the customer wants to do business with. Customer preference is a powerful differentiator. When the customer wants to work with you, and believes your organization is the one they can most effectively *partner* with, you can often win the business even if your fit isn't the strongest or your value the most unique. Customers are people, too, and it's likely that they consider the strong alignment they have developed with you and your team to be valuable to their business.

Remember, your ability to differentiate is enabled by your application of Strategies 1 through 7, and the work you've done thus far. Now you can use the actionable awareness you gained through discovery, the trust-based relationships you built in alignment, and the mindshare you created with your positioning efforts. You'll make the distinctions clear to your customer through the fit of your solutions, the uniqueness of your value, and the partnership you can provide.

Planning to win is about helping your customer see greater value in what you have to offer. You might think of this as your *value edge*, the difference between the value you propose to deliver to your customer and what your competitor proposes. If you don't have a value edge, you're at risk and you should probably get comfortable with being commoditized; when there's no value edge, there's no differentiation because your customer doesn't see (or at least acknowledge) a difference. Relationships don't matter. Preference is not a concern. Pick one solution or another; it's all the same. And if you don't have a value edge, you better brace for impact: you're planning to lose.

In today's complex and stressful selling environment, you must have a value edge, and it should be based on more than product features and price. Just as importantly, the customer should be able to recognize and acknowledge the difference in the value you offer. To be compelling, your value difference must be:

- **Much stronger than product features,** because everybody's got product features, and in many cases, the customer can't tell which ones are better.

- **More powerful than the product benefits** that every supplier (including you) claims to have. Benefits are subjective and will always yield to the effective differentiation of unique business value.

- **Sustainable**, meaning that your customer should believe that if they work with you, they will be better off because what you do for them will have enduring value. Your value edge reaches far beyond the "feature of the day" or the "benefit of the week" because it will withstand the test of time.

- **Valuable to the customer,** which literally means "able to be of value." You'll find this in items that are measurable, sustainable, stronger than features, and more powerful than benefits. And what could possibly be more measurable and sustainable than value that enables the customer to meet their business objectives and be successful?

Defining your value edge means creating space between you and your competition. To do this, you must leverage the customer mindshare you've developed through your effective positioning and the trust that has been created through your alignment.

Developing the Ideal Environment for Value Differentiation

If your value differentiation is to be effective, you need to leverage the work that you have already done with your customer. This means that the ideal environment for effective value differentiation will be a function of the insight and actionable awareness that you have gathered as a result of your discovery efforts, the relationships that you have developed as a result of the alignment between your team and your customer's team, and the customer mindshare that has become your real estate as a result of your effective positioning. Ideally, you want your customer to believe, as they look at other providers, that your organization offers more value to their business, and even better, more *unique* business value.

The challenge now is to expand your customer mindshare into customer *preference*, which is achievable when it follows effective discovery, alignment, and positioning, but nearly impossible when it's attempted in a vacuum. Without these three in place, your efforts to differentiate can seem hollow, boastful, and even arrogant. You haven't earned the right, so the message doesn't resonate.

Your customer has multiple ways to evaluate your organization. They can measure you in terms of your products, resources, expertise, services, customer experience, and your brand/reputation. We covered all six in Strategy 7, but we did so in terms of mindshare. Now we take it to the next level and extend the context of that conversation into the realm of value— unique, measurable business value.

If "value" refers to those things that you provide that matter most to your customer, then "unique value" takes it a step further. When your value is unique, your customer believes that you are going to do a better job of providing it than anyone else.

Let's look at the six components of positioning (see Figure 7-1) in terms of value and unique value:

- **Products.** *The customer believes that your products are superior to your competitors' products.*

    In terms of unique value, the clock is the enemy of the product. Customers today find it considerably more difficult to see product differences than they did in the past. Product development cycle times have gotten significantly shorter. If you offer something that a competing supplier doesn't, it's fairly easy for that competitor to say, "Give us until Monday (or next week, or next month), and we'll offer it, too." Dave has consulted with technology companies that won't even begin to build certain new products until they have achieved, in advance, a threshold level of sales, promising something better to compete against rivals that already provide a similar product. Differentiation based on product superiority can be fragile, frequently short-lived, and often ineffective, unless there are profound and sustainable differences between products.

- **Resources.** *The customer believes your people and technology will enable their success.*

  When resources enter the mix, things get more interesting. On the positioning side, you want your customer's team members to feel comfortable with the people they interact with from your organization. At the value level, you want your customer to believe that your people, your technology, and your infrastructure will enable their success. If your alignment has been effective, you already know exactly how your customer defines success.

- **Expertise.** *The customer believes your people are knowledgeable, credible, and able to share relevant best practices.*

  Expertise is a hot topic these days. A significant number of organizations consider expertise to be *the* big differentiator in today's selling environment. We don't want to put words into your customer's mouth, but we increasingly find that knowledgeable customers value expertise—not just resources, but expert resources. There's a difference, and that's very important to note. Your alignment with your customer has helped you establish trust and credibility, and you now have a chance to further differentiate through your subject matter expertise.

- **Services.** *The customer believes your service levels are higher and more proactive.*

  Few organizations sell a product in isolation; there's almost always a service component. Your customer perceives value when your services are offered more proactively and at higher levels, when they're more substantial, and when accessing them isn't stressful. When you combine services with resources and expertise, your ability to demonstrate true uniqueness is stronger because your unique value is based on specific resources and people that are exclusive to you and your organization.

- **Customer Experience.** *The customer believes that your work and experience with comparable organizations reduces their risk.*

  This can also refer to your experience with comparable solution types or in the customer's industry. In some parts of the world, it may mean similar geographies; many customers like to buy from organizations that have done business locally, whether it's a region, country, or even a city. The idea is that the customer finds your customer experience and your industry experience valuable, and perceives that their risk is reduced because of contributions you've made to other businesses in the past.

- **Brand/reputation.** *The customer believes in your reputation for quality, service, and product excellence, and you derive competitive advantage as a result.*

  In Strategy 7, we explored the difference between brand and reputation. Brand is brand; it might get you in the door once, but many customers won't buy from you a second time if your product or service doesn't live up to expectations. Reputation becomes a differentiator when your customer's previous experience with what you and your organization have delivered in the past has been positive. When reputation is acting in your favor, you have a very powerful differentiator, indeed.

Have You Earned the Right to Differentiate? Let's review the steps we've taken so far, as well as the critical role each plays in developing the right environment for effective differentiation.

Although discovery isn't something that only occurs during the sale, you began Section II by finding out what's going on in your customer's world—beyond reading an RFP. The reward for your discovery efforts is the ability to connect your solutions back to your customer's issues, indicating that doing business with you will help them solve their challenges and be successful. And because your discovery revealed what your customer's business objectives are, you know precisely what your unique value needs to connect with, which you wouldn't have known otherwise. Even when your features and benefits add up to a strong solution, your customer won't value it as much if it doesn't clearly help them meet their business objectives and, ultimately, address their external drivers.

In alignment, you worked to build relationships, and you now have supporters and, more importantly, sponsors within your customer's organization. It's true that many factors contribute to a sales win or loss, but the role of sponsors in differentiation is significant. Having sponsors (or even a strong supporter) can amplify your differentiation in powerful ways. Sponsors can do the following:

- **Provide you with information and insight that you don't have and can't get otherwise.** They want to help you because you have delivered some level of past proven value to them or another company, and they believe that their risk is reduced by selecting you.

- **Serve as an internal advocate for you and your company.** You can't be with your customer all the time, and your position in the account will absolutely be challenged when you aren't around. An effective sponsor is willing and able to vouch for you in your absence, and possibly even debrief with you afterwards.

- **Remove obstacles and roadblocks that you might not be able to remove on your own.** This begins with your knowledge of the obstacles and roadblocks—and who hasn't been in sales situations where you felt that you were spinning your wheels with no progress? Your sponsor not only ensures that you are aware of potential blocking factors, but can also help you move or at least address those factors so that you can make progress.

- **Provide ongoing coaching and advice.** The effective application of knowledge is power in most environments, and sales is certainly no exception. The sponsor that provides coaching and advice equips you to make the best choices and establish the right priorities, enabling differentiation to occur that otherwise would be impossible.

- **Provide references for you after the sale.** References are earned for a number of reasons, not the least of which is past proven value. An effective sponsor is not only willing to help you internally, within his or her own organization, but also externally, with a customer or prospect who wants to hear from other customers about your performance.

- **Help you grow a business relationship into an effective partnership.** Sponsors are, in fact, the source of most partnerships.

Think about your own experience with customers that consider you more than just another vendor. You almost certainly had a sponsor who cared enough to help grow that relationship with you. Now look at a sales outcome that went the wrong way. Did you get that result because you "didn't know what you didn't know" until it was too late to learn? When you have a sponsor, the likelihood of this happening is dramatically reduced.

The bridge between alignment and differentiation is positioning. This can be summed up fairly simply: If you don't position before you differentiate, you're asking your customer to believe that you are the best before they fully understand what you provide and how it addresses their challenges. Positioning sets the table so you can articulate your value and differentiate your *unique* value. It also helps your customer's team members gain a full understanding of what you can do for them. Effective positioning benefits both the seller and the buyer, and it paves the way for differentiation.

With this in mind, it's easy to see that *differentiation* is a function of your discovery, alignment, and positioning, and the order in which you deploy these skills matters. Think of

Discovery → Alignment → Positioning → Differentiation

as a more modern alternative to the traditional approach to sales process, which tends to be focused on inflexible stages and steps. Beginning with discovery and evolving into differentiation, this provides a contemporary plan to win based on proven skills and best practices. Best of all, it can be synchronized much more intuitively with how your customer buys than the rigid sales process models that have haunted salespeople and account managers for decades.

When competitive differentiation is fueled by effective discovery, alignment, and positioning, something powerful happens. Discovery provides you with the insight and actionable awareness to initiate the planning to win process. It helps you understand what's most important to your customer and what they value most: their external drivers, business objectives, internal challenges, and success criteria.

Alignment makes the connections between your sales/account team and your customer's decision team, as well as between your solutions and your customer's internal challenges. It establishes a conduit between how your customer defines success and the solutions and value that you will deliver. Perhaps most importantly, it is the basis for establishing credibility and developing trust-based relationships with your customer, which are important to every customer we have ever interviewed.

Positioning helps to ensure that your customer's perception of you and your organization is strong and that they recognize the solutions, advantages, and value that you can provide. Through effective positioning, you are able to raise your dialogue with the customer and ensure that you and your offering are a critical component of their vision of success. Effective positioning establishes critical customer mindshare for you, and the solutions, advantages, and value that your organization will provide.

Differentiation is a function of all three. Take out the insight and actionable awareness gained in discovery and you weaken your potential to differentiate. Remove the credibility and trust-based relationships you developed through alignment and you weaken your potential to differentiate. Without the mindshare and elevated conversations on which you based your positioning, your potential to differentiate is weakened. But when discovery, alignment, and positioning are effectively executed, the result is a powerful platform for competitive differentiation and a strong likelihood that your plan to win will become a reality.

To make a point, let's reverse the order of the skills that we discussed earlier:

Differentiation → *Positioning* → *Alignment* → *Discovery*

The process becomes almost comical, because in reverse, it begins with you trying to create a preference and helping the customer see your competitive advantages. After this fails, you would try to position your solution by developing customer mindshare and creating a positive perception. This won't work because the customer doesn't know you. So, with any credibility that may remain, you'd have to try and connect to build a trust-based relationship through alignment, which will certainly fall flat. Finally, if the customer is still speaking to you, you'd probably head into the discovery phase and attempt to find out what's important to them and learn a bit about what's going on in their world.

Absurd? Definitely! But unfortunately, it's the approach taken by too many salespeople—and it's just the kind of behavior that tarnishes the reputation of the sales profession.

Planning to win means that you plan your sales approach in terms of a logical sequence based on how the customer is thinking. Looked at this way, it becomes apparent that this approach fits practically all buying processes, even those involving RFPs. When your discovery, alignment, positioning, and differentiation (in that order) are effective, something powerful is going on. In any given opportunity, only one or two providers actually get high marks in each of the four strategies. Make sure that you are highly effective in each and watch your likelihood of winning increase.

Think Like the Competition. In Strategy 7, we suggested that your competitors will be actively trying to advance their own positioning and counter-positioning strategies. As a result, it's important to anticipate what they might be up to. Granted, thinking like a competitor can be trickier for organizations in some markets than others, and certain industries just seem to be more competitively aware than others. But thinking like the competition is a process that all salespeople and account managers should be able to deploy.

You may have heard the expression, "Whoever says it first says it best." We agree. It means you shouldn't wait until your competitor puts you at a disadvantage to begin to leverage and discuss your competitive strengths with your customer. This concept can be readily observed in the political world when one side or another sets the narrative around a hot issue, compelling the other side to react and respond.

At the end of the day, you cannot expect your customer—who is relentlessly bombarded by information, chronically crunched for time, and under persistent pressure from a variety of fronts—to see any difference between you and the others if you can't point it out explicitly. Steve once heard a salesperson comment, "Well, you would think they could see the difference." We wouldn't think that at all, and you shouldn't either. There's every reason to assume that your customer is not going to see your unique value if you do not clearly differentiate and articulate your value edge. If you've never spelled out your specific strengths, advantages, and differences, why would your customer know that you have any?

Activities for Effective Differentiation

In terms of sales execution, differentiation can occur in a variety of places. While there is at least some potential for it every time you engage with your customer, some of the most effective differentiation occurs later in the evolution of an opportunity.

Consider the following activities as ideal for differentiating yourself. As you read, think about the last competitive opportunity that you worked, and ask yourself how well you did in each area.

- **Validating your customer-specific value proposition with the customer's decision team, and adjusting it as needed.**

  What matters here is that you develop a value proposition for your customer that is specific to their business and the opportunity at hand. Based on your understanding of their external drivers, business objectives, and internal challenges, you are able to talk about the types of solutions and advantages you offer. You can discuss your successes with comparable organizations and the unique value that you and your organization will deliver.

Remember that when you are validating your value proposition, you have the opportunity to ask your customer for feedback. If you're on the wrong side of the value edge, it's better to know sooner than later.

- **Differentiating your unique value with key members of the customer's decision team.**

    You can't help a company see what makes you unique. You don't talk to a *company*; you talk to *people* on the decision team. These team members each have professional and personal needs, wants, and reasons for the decisions they make. If you can't connect your value with one of these, you're missing a tremendous opportunity to differentiate at an individual or personal level.

- **Verifying and providing references and success stories to your customer's decision team.**

    References and success stories are woefully underutilized in selling today. People talk about them, but postmortems on lost opportunities show referencing and the use of success stories are not as widespread they once were, or should be. Casual mention is just not good enough. The whole idea of providing a reference (and doing so before the competition does) is to assure your customer that they are safe doing business with you by reducing their sense of risk. They don't have to take your word for it; they can hear what another customer—a specific person at a particular company—has to say.

    The most important question a savvy customer will ask your reference is, "If you had to do it again, would you make the same decision?" Before your customer makes that call, you should know how your reference will answer that question.

- **Conducting an executive sponsor call and validating your winning position.**

  By definition, your executive sponsor wants you to win. Having alignment with a sponsor at high level within your customer's organization means that you can confirm where you are, what you've learned, whether your value proposition has been validated, and whether you're in a strong position to win. Armed with this competitive insight, good follow-up questions include: "Why do you feel that way?" "If I have a weakness, where is it?" and "If the evaluation ended today, where would I stand?"

- **Developing a final proposal and reviewing it with your customer's decision team.**

  By calling out the specific areas that you know are important, the proposal review becomes an exercise in differentiation. You know what's important because you spoke with your customer, did your discovery, aligned around what was most critical to them, and positioned your solutions, advantages, and value. The objective of this discussion is to test your proposal, looking for strengths and weaknesses via individual feedback from your customer's decision team members, and then adjust as appropriate.

- **Securing customer notification of your selection.**

  When your customer tells you that you have been selected, it's nice to hear, but it's just as important to ask why. You want this answer for a couple of reasons. First, you're probably curious and should know the reason. Second, until a formal decision is made and agreements are signed, you haven't really won the business. It's one thing for the customer to say you've been selected, but until you get a commitment, there's always a possibility that something will go wrong. That said, when you hear from the customer that you're in the lead, it's a good place to be.

Sometimes sellers grumble that they offer more value than the customer gives them credit for. Not too long ago, Steve even heard a sales executive say, "I'm tired of being cherry-picked on value by my customers." Digging into that statement further, Steve got to the bottom of what the executive meant, which was essentially, "Customers want all the value, but they also want the best price. If we try to bring the price down by cutting something out, they won't accept that either!"

To overcome this frustrating situation, you have to be able to develop and deliver a strong value message. Think about where you are in your market. Are you selling to companies that are interested in learning more about the value you propose to deliver? If not, take another look, and ask yourself if you're investing time in the right accounts. Most customers will want to hear about your value, especially if it's unique and can enable their success.

Proving Your Value: Building Customer-Specific Value Messages

In Strategy 5, we introduced you to the concepts of external drivers, business objectives, and internal challenges. In Strategy 6, we looked at ways to align with the customer, connecting your team with the customer's team and building trust-based relationships. In Strategy 7, we examined positioning in terms of fit and the capture of customer mindshare around your solutions and advantages. Now in Strategy 8, we've shown you how to differentiate your unique value. The customer-specific value proposition framework (Figure 8-1) is a tool designed to facilitate your value communication. This framework brings it all together in a compact format that is easy to use and remember. Simple and intuitive, it can also be used to summarize your value for the purpose of an internal account team discussion, provide a value summary for your customer proposal, and, as you will see in Section III, provide the structure for engaging your customer in conversations about your past proven value.

The Power of Unique Value. We've talked a lot in this chapter about value, unique value, and the importance of differentiating yourself in these terms rather than by way of such factors as product and price—but what exactly does *unique differentiable value* mean? "Unique" means that you

A FRAMEWORK TO COMMUNICATE YOUR UNIQUE VALUE	
Customer's External Drivers	What external drivers and pressures are impacting your customer's business?
Customer's Business Objectives	What is your customer doing to address their external drivers?
Customer's Internal Challenges	What could prevent your customer from meeting their business objectives?
Your Solutions	How will you work together with your customer to resolve their internal challenges?
Your Advantages	How are you different from your competition in resolving these internal challenges?
Your Successes	Which other customers have you helped resolve similar internal challenges?
Your Unique Value	How have you created value that has helped your customer achieve their objectives and address their drivers?

Figure 8-1. **A framework to communicate your unique value.**

can deliver a type of value to your customer that no one else can. "Differentiable value" means you are capable of distinguishing the uniqueness of your value in the six areas that we discussed earlier, and that your customer recognizes and acknowledges it. Communicating with your customer about value is extremely important; otherwise, how will they know there's a difference between you and others, or understand what that difference means to them? How will they feel the impact of your value edge?

Sales transformation leader and Senior Director of Sales Enablement for Brainshark, Mike Kunkle, a widely heard and well-respected authority on sales performance improvement, has this perspective:

"We've been hearing a lot of talk about value creation. Sales research (from SiriusDecisions, Forrester, and others) shows that the inability to communicate value is one of the greatest inhibitors to sales growth. From my seat on the bus, though, I see the inability to communicate value as only part of the problem. I believe the deeper issue is the inability to create value."

Consider the word *valuable*. When the customer finds you "value-able" in ways that they don't find anyone else valuable, and those areas of value connect directly with what's most important to them, you have something very powerful. So when you bring it all to the table—your products, re-sources, expertise, services, customer experience, and brand/reputation—in the form of solutions and unique value, you help the customer see how you and your organization can help them resolve their internal challenges and achieve their business objectives. When this happens, you have com-piled it for the customer in a compact format that makes it clear and understandable.

Notice, as you move through the seven-step framework outlined in Fig-ure 8-2, that you begin with discovery, move into alignment, then on to positioning, and finally to differentiation. The application of these skills

Figure 8-2. A powerful sequence for engaging differently with your customer.

forms a powerful sequence for both you and your customer, and the framework helps you evolve your data and information into insight and actionable awareness, exactly where you want and need to be when you're planning to win. In the end, you help your customer see what makes you and your organization different. It's all about value: your unique differentiable value.

Engaging Your Customer in Value Conversations. We're all familiar with the old adage, "A picture is worth a thousand words." Perhaps this is why the value conversation process lends itself so easily to graphical representation. Allowing you to engage your customer in a visual conversation around your unique differentiable value, Figure 8-3 can be sketched out—live—using a whiteboard, flipchart, tablet device, or even the back of a cocktail napkin. It works even better when you get your customer's team members involved, because they can literally draw the connections between their challenges and your solutions, and their objectives and your value. When you go through this exercise with them, don't be surprised if

Figure 8-3. Facilitating value conversations with your customer.

they ask you not to erase or discard the completed value message, because they want to keep it for future reference. It happens all the time.

The primary goal of a value conversation is to engage differently and show your customer how your solutions help them resolve their internal challenges, and how your unique value enables them to meet and exceed their business objectives. When you are successful in doing this, there's a good chance they will notice that someone is talking with them in a very different way. You may be the only one among your set of competitors who engages like this, and by being the one who's most effective, you become part of your own value edge.

Value differentiation is very special. It can put you in a strong place as you move into *after the sale*. Differentiation shows that you understand what your customer's value expectations are and your level of commitment to their success. When this happens, don't be surprised if you hear your customer say, "No one has talked to me this way before, and I like it!"

Testing the Effectiveness of Your Value Differentiation

The following six sets of questions will help you evaluate the strength of your value differentiation with your customer:

1. **Are you better positioned with your customer's approvers, decision makers, recommenders, and influencers than your competition?** If so, what evidence do you have? If not, why don't you know?

2. **Does your customer believe that you offer a stronger solution fit than your competitors?** If so, how can you be sure? If not, how are you going to change this perception?

3. **Have you provided your customer with proof of your ability to create and co-create measurable business value?** If so, what is it and how did the customer react? How and when will you demonstrate the superiority of your value or other key metrics important to your customer?

4. **Have you developed and validated your customer-specific value proposition with your customer?** If so, what is it and how did you validate it with the customer? If not, with whatever time is left, what are you going to do step-by-step?

5. **Are your customer sponsors and supporters able to articulate your unique value within their organization?** Who are they and what's in it for them? How do you know they understand and can articulate your unique value? Why will they go to bat for you if your price is higher or your terms more demanding?

6. **Does your customer's vision of meeting their objectives align with your value/unique value?** How have you helped them see precisely how your value/unique value connects with their objectives for this opportunity? Why do they believe that you and your organization will provide value that will better enable them to meet and exceed their objectives than any of your competitors?

Case Studies

Adecco Staffing U.S.

Based in Switzerland, Adecco S.A. is a Fortune Global 500 company and the world leader in workforce solutions. Each day, it connects over 650,000 associates with more than 100,000 business clients through its network of over 33,000 employees and 5,500 offices in more than 60 countries. Adecco Staffing U.S. is a leading provider of recruitment and workforce solutions, offering services in the areas of temporary staffing and permanent placement to a wide variety of organizations.

Adecco assists customers with projects that can require anywhere from a few to a few hundred people at a time. Customers rely on the company to recruit and place their temporary personnel ("associates") to assist with seasonal needs or special projects, or, on an ongoing basis, to help provide more flexibility and cost savings in their workforce. Because Adecco Staffing is in the business of placing people, customer engagement is critical to helping recruit the right talent. Joyce Russell, President of Adecco Staffing U.S., is firmly committed to customer relationships and had this to say about the importance of effective customer engagement: "In business, relationships are everything, and effective customer engagement creates relationships that are based on trust and a commitment to a shared vision.

Having trust-based relationships with the customer is the first step in building a long-term successful business partnership."

Customer Engagement: What Adecco Does to Effectively Engage Customers

Taking a "customer-centric" approach is not new to Adecco. According to Andrea Sugden, Executive Vice President of Sales and National Accounts, Adecco Staffing's sales teams have always taken a "customer first" approach. "We've historically done a very good job of making sure we focus on relationships throughout the sales cycle, and not letting our processes distract us," Sugden explains. "Both are important, but our business really dictates that we know our customer well enough to recruit and select the right talent and help them plan ahead for large scale projects."

However, like most businesses in the years that preceded the recent recession, which began in 2008, Adecco found itself facing such external drivers as increased competition, pricing pressures, and more complex requests from customers. This new competitive landscape required the company to expand its service offerings and increase the size of its strategic account teams to meet growing customer demands. Most of the teams that supported strategic global customers grew, some from only a handful to dozens of people who would ultimately add value to the account. As a result, larger sales and account teams from several divisions were required to collaborate and work together more cohesively than in years past. In addition, due to numerous acquisitions within its brand portfolio, the organization's sales leaders recognized that no single sales or customer engagement methodology existed across the enterprise. In short, Adecco needed to find a way to maintain their "customer-centric" approach while being able to scale it for larger account teams, as well as for larger and more complex customer teams.

Adecco's leadership recognized this challenge and made a strategic decision to adopt a common sales and customer engagement methodology throughout the organization. The company's leadership wanted to grow without losing their "high-touch" or "boutique" approach. "It wasn't enough to just hire customer-centric people," Sugden explains. "We basically needed to learn how to scale up relationship building for larger accounts."

Adecco's new customer engagement initiative began in 2008 with several workshops for executives, sales leadership, and account managers throughout the company. The newly selected methodology provided a common language and framework for account teams to work together and communicate more effectively internally, which enabled them to communicate more effectively externally with customers.

Adecco's sales leaders worked closely with their Learning and Development team to facilitate ongoing workshops, and together they created a follow-up and coaching program to help reinforce the new methodology. Adecco's Strategic Sales Support team (a marketing and proposal writing resource team) attended workshops as well, to create more alignment with field sales. Lastly, the company took critical components of the new customer engagement methodology and embedded them in Salesforce.com to assist with sales and pipeline management. Adecco's commitment to the program remained strong, and demand for workshop attendance and coaching increased steadily during the 18 to 24 months following the program launch.

Engagement Excellence: How Adecco Gets It Right for Customers

Through their new customer engagement and coaching programs, Adecco's sales teams learned how to more effectively collaborate and engage internally. They could engage with their customer more successfully because team insight regarding the customer's business was more accurate and comprehensive. These teams became far more effective at "value-focused selling" by creating customer-specific value propositions. The company's sales organization continues to involve their Strategic Sales Support team as well, to ensure that everyone involved in the sales process (from early engagement to final proposal) truly understands what the customer is trying to achieve by engaging with Adecco. As a result, the company's written correspondence (cover letters, executive summaries, presentations, etc.) has become far more customer-focused than ever before.

Adecco's sales leadership recognizes the importance of a customer-centric approach throughout the entire customer relationship. "One of the things we have done well is to make sure that our efforts with the customer before, during, and after the sale are all tied together and not done in isolation or in silos," Sugden says. "It's important that our customers experience consistency every time they engage with Adecco, wherever they may be in their decision processes and procurement cycles."

To reinforce the importance of this strategy, Adecco Staffing has aligned sales, implementation, and account management under the same leadership. This has proven to be invaluable to the company in winning new customers and retaining them after the sale. This approach provides the customer with continuity and assures that what is "sold" is actually implemented and delivered. The organization has also seen the benefits of this structure because it allows leadership to build strong relationships with customers and assign implementation and account teams that are the best cultural and organizational fit.

The Impact: Why Engagement Excellence Matters to Adecco's Customers

Adecco was an industry leader even prior to adopting a unified sales and customer engagement methodology. However, the new program has made a significant impact. Adecco Staffing was closing or winning approximately 10 to 15 percent of its RFPs prior to adopting the new methodology, but leadership saw steady improvement—exceeding a 65 percent RFP "win rate"—in 2013 and 2014, and continued to beat the market in top-line sales. Over the same period, Adecco has also decreased the time investment required to go from propose to win (final presentation to contract signed) from 180 days to 118 days as a direct result of the new sales and customer engagement methodology. Sugden attributes this to improved relationships with their customers before and during the sales process, and to being more selective about which RFPs and customers to pursue. "It's more important to align with customers where we find mutual value because it makes the relationship far more rewarding for both parties," she says.

"When we achieve this level of trust and transparency with customers early in the process, the result is more value creation for the customer because we really know what they need. I believe this is critical throughout the customer relationship cycle."

Procter & Gamble (P&G), a strategic customer of Adecco Staffing, agrees on the importance of a strong customer-supplier relationship. Mario Perez Castillo of P&G Procurement manages the relationship between P&G's global headquarters and the Adecco Staffing P&G team. He had this to say about the relationship between P&G and Adecco:

> "Adecco's Cincinnati team is a business partner that has been supportive in our day-to-day quest of delivery and to retain the most qualified and well-suited associates for our global headquarters and Technology Centers. One of the reasons they are so successful with us is because they have really taken the time to learn and understand what P&G needs on many different levels. Our program with Adecco has grown into a fully automated and sophisticated process which continues to evolve as the business climate changes. Consistent, excellent delivery with strategic vision alignment between P&G and Adecco has been key for our business and this is what sets them apart."

Rhonda Arledge, Adecco's Regional Vice President, who manages the company's relationship with P&G, offers additional insight about Adecco's approach to customer engagement: "We learned that there is no single value proposition or solution that applies to every customer. In fact, I think it's safe to say we all learned to stop selling first, and instead learn more about our customer, and then try to determine how we can best help them. This approach has helped us grow stronger relationships with strategic customers like P&G."

The Takeaways: Why This Matters to You

Customer engagement excellence takes time and begins well before the sale. Adecco embraced the idea that sales teams must be aligned as a team first before engaging with the customer. Team alignment before the sale leads to better alignment with the customer during and after the sale. Further, creating a cultural change in a sales organization requires commitment from the top down. The Adecco initiative started with its senior leadership, and cascaded down and across the organization with partnership from the Learning and Development, Marketing, and Strategic Sales Support teams. It was important to Adecco leadership that this initiative expand well beyond a workshop, and become part of their sales and customer engagement framework.

Adecco has remained committed to their sales and customer engagement methodology, and it has become embedded into their culture. It's far too common in business to try new approaches without providing the necessary resources, reinforcement, or time needed to allow for success. It's clear from the results that Adecco is getting it right.

This example underscores the importance of moving beyond individual sales execution, and shows the importance of account team alignment and execution with strategic customers. It emphasizes that complex sales organizations can grow while keeping customer relationships at the heart of every initiative. Adecco has firmly bought into the notion that it really is all about the customer: before, during, and after the sale.

Honeywell Building Solutions

Honeywell Building Solutions (HBS), a strategic business unit of Honeywell, delivers technologies that address some of the world's most difficult challenges. These include energy efficiency, clean energy generation, safety and security, globalization, and customer productivity specifically within the building environment.

HBS installs, integrates, and maintains the systems that keep facilities safe, secure, comfortable, productive, and energy efficient—from building automation and management solutions that increase facility performance to security and life safety solutions that help mitigate risk. HBS works with thousands of commercial, industrial, municipal, federal, and utility customers worldwide to identify challenges and to provide customized solutions that provide the data its customers need to make better facility decisions.

Customer Engagement: What HBS Does to Effectively Engage Customers

HBS has learned that the key to providing customers with improved intelligence lies in the integration of systems, which makes it easier for a customer to be provided with visibility, access, and control over all aspects of a building. Similarly, HBS believes in applying an integrated approach to managing its customer relationships and ensuring that customers have an exceptional experience throughout their relationship with the company. Kevin Madden, General Manager for the HBS Energy Services Group, puts it this way: "We believe it is critical to get the right people at HBS doing the right things for the customer from the very beginning of each potential new opportunity, and to work with intensity and urgency on the things that matter to customers the most." Kevin displays both a compass and a clock in his office as visual reminders that the keys to success with customers are alignment (both internally and externally), and working with intensity and urgency to get the right things done for them as quickly and efficiently as possible. HBS' pursuit of continuous process improvement is not just limited to its products and services; it is also evident in its pursuit of excellent engagement with customers.

Engagement Excellence: How HBS Gets It Right for Customers

To ensure focus on the right things *during* the sales process, HBS has implemented a number of best practices designed to improve the customer experience from the earliest stages of customer engagement. Sean Mahoney, Vice President of Sales for HBS Americas, offers this perspective:

> "If we're going to be able to position our solutions and differentiate our value with our customers, it's critically important that we invest the time early in each sale to understand what our customers are trying to do and why they need our help. Early discovery and alignment with our customers provide a strong foundation upon which we can demonstrate that we are authentic in our attempts to create unique value with our customers."

One best practice that continues to make a difference with HBS is the internal weekly meeting, where cross-functional teams and HBS leadership discuss the criteria for new potential sales opportunities, including:

- **Customer-Specific Value Proposition.** Defined to ensure that everyone knows what specific problem or challenge HBS is trying to solve for the customer.

- **Identification of Sponsors and Supporters.** By both HBS and the customer to ensure that support for the initiative is provided at the highest levels on each side.

- **Procurement Process/Decision Schedule.** Outlined and discussed.

- **Strategy to Win.** Outlined and discussed.

In addition, a whiteboard approach is used in collaborative discovery and planning sessions with customers. HBS emphasizes that one key to their success has been ensuring a focus on new sales opportunities in which the customer shows a commitment to collaborate to collectively identify and overcome obstacles. These "customer-facing" whiteboard collaboration meetings typically include:

- **Customer Objectives and Challenges.** Illustrating visually that HBS understands what the customer is trying to accomplish.

- **HBS Solutions.** Illustrating visually which HBS solutions will help address the customer's objectives and challenges.

- **Decision Schedule.** Outlined and discussed for updates or changes on both sides.

- **Potential Obstacles.** Outlined in three categories (financial, contractual, and technical) with collaborative discussions to address solutions.

Sue Arbisi, Sales Development Leader for HBS Americas, offers additional insight regarding the power of this approach:

"We've had customers use our whiteboard approach to communicate value within their own organizations—the same approach that we used to collaborate with them in our value discovery process. They've found it to be a powerful technique for positioning and communicating their business value (and the value HBS can help them create) with their internal colleagues. This approach to value articulation and collaboration drives higher levels of customer engagement and has proven to be a strong differentiator for us."

The Impact: Why Engagement Excellence Matters to HBS' Customers

To drive higher levels of collaboration and innovation, HBS provides customers with dedicated account team resources, whose function is to learn everything possible about the customer and connect the appropriate solutions with the customer's needs. This helps create synergy and alignment internally within HBS, and establishes an integrated approach to managing customer relationships.

This best practice is demonstrated in the relationship between HBS and The Dow Chemical Company. HBS and Dow have done business together for many years, and the level of value creation and co-creation between the organizations has been significant. Tim Scott, Chief Security Officer and Global Director for Emergency Service and Security at Dow, explains:

> "Dow and HBS have worked together on Dow's security systems for over 25 years—starting with a typical customer-vendor relationship focused on site-by-site needs and system implementation at a few sites in the U.S. to what is today a robust partnership with global reach. A true partnership recognizes the goals and needs of both parties and ensures the success of both through open communication and teamwork. While there are always bumps along the way, Dow and HBS have achieved a successful partnership and this partnership is the foundation for our global leadership in the world of chemical industry security."

By implementing strategies for more effective customer engagement, HBS has focused their selling efforts on how customers define value. In addition, relationships with strategic customers have improved significantly and continue to grow. Julio Ampuero, HBS' Integrated Security Solutions Leader, offers this perspective:

> "Our business is providing security solutions to many of the largest companies in the world. To do this successfully, it's critical that we are able to connect the value that HBS can provide to the specific requirements and needs of our customers. When this happens, we are able to differentiate ourselves not only through our products and technologies, but also through the way that we engage with our clients."

The Takeaway: Why This Matters to You

HBS' sales and account teams must "earn the right to engage" with customers early in the sales process. To accomplish this, HBS sales management and leadership have equipped their customer-facing employees with tools and best practices to help them understand what their customers are trying to accomplish before proposing solutions.

While some of these tools and best practices may appear, on the surface, to be tactical, the impact on HBS' business has been anything but superficial. This approach to excellent customer engagement serves now as a strategic "compass" for both HBS and its customers throughout the sales process and beyond, resulting in increased levels of customer collaboration, alignment, and ultimately, trusted advisor status where business is mutually beneficial. Global Account Executive Dave Olson, who is responsible for HBS' business with Dow, has this to say:

> "We've learned that our success with strategic customers like Dow can be directly attributed to our knowledge of their business. We invest significant time internally at HBS, making sure our team truly understands what Dow is trying to accomplish, and what challenges they might face in trying to achieve their goals. This enables us to work collaboratively with Dow and co-develop best practices, processes, and global offerings. Then we can we create real value by making the appropriate connections between their business challenges and our solutions."

HBS' excellent engagement with Dow demonstrates what can happen when a commitment to discover and understand the customer leads to increased levels of alignment and partnership between seller and buyer. Through value conversations that align objectives and effectively position and differentiate their value, HBS can operate with laser focus on the things that matter most to customers before, during, and after each sale.

Panasonic

Panasonic Corporation, a multinational electronics corporation headquartered in Osaka, Japan, is committed to improving the lives of people around the world. The company is globally recognized for consumer products such as TVs, home appliances, and digital cameras, as well as commercial solutions for heating, refrigeration, and air conditioning. With net sales of more than $64 billion and over 270,000 employees worldwide, Panasonic includes 505 consolidated companies, including the parent company.

The strength of Panasonic's brand has been developed and sustained over nearly 100 years since Konosuke Matsushita founded the company in 1918. Prior to becoming a global consumer electronics powerhouse, Panasonic developed component and material technologies that continue to serve as building blocks for the wide range of advanced products the company is best known for today. Panasonic technology is also deeply embedded in many products developed by Panasonic partners around the globe, from refrigerator compressors to the components and batteries found in mobile devices.

Bringing strategic innovation and industrial technology to customers, Panasonic Industrial Devices Sales Company of America is a division of Panasonic Corporation of America. Panasonic Industrial Devices offers industrial electronic components, energy solutions, industrial automation, and infrastructure solutions. Partners use the label "Powered by Panasonic" to convey that Panasonic technology is embedded in their product. Panasonic views this demonstration of confidence and trust as a critical measure of success. Jeff Howell, President of Panasonic Industrial Devices, offers this perspective:

> "We're proud and honored to provide our customers with the performance, quality, and reliability they depend on to build world-class solutions for their customers. We strive to develop collaborative strategic partnerships with our customers based on understanding their needs, identifying synergies, and providing a wide breadth of Panasonic resources, capabilities, and products so that together

we can create solutions that improve the lives of people around the globe."

Customer Engagement: What Panasonic Does to Effectively Engage Customers

Dedicated to putting the customer first, Panasonic Industrial Devices ensures that each member of its cross-functional team of sales, product management, engineering, and manufacturing has a deep understanding of customer requirements throughout each engagement. Experience has shown that when everyone is clear about how the customer will use the product, the timeframes required to meet and exceed expectations, and anticipated demand and production levels, the Panasonic team's ability to meet the needs of the customer improves dramatically.

An example of this philosophy in action is the Energy Sales division, which produces battery packs and specialty batteries that are embedded in their customers' products. This division also provides technical expertise to help their customers' engineers design highly reliable performance technology into their products. Additionally, they offer rigorous manufacturing and testing standards, delivering a host of information to the customer during the product development process, and their "localized engineering" service model provides real-time technical expertise when and where it's needed. Panasonic sales professionals are responsible for every aspect of the customer relationship, providing a single point of contact for contracting, specifications, pricing, and logistics.

Engagement Excellence: How Panasonic Gets It Right for Customers

Panasonic's customer, Streamlight, Inc., produces portable lighting equipment for fire, rescue, law enforcement, automotive, industrial, sporting goods, and the military—people whose jobs and lives can depend on having a reliable light source. The company's slogan is "Heroes Trust Streamlight."

Streamlight was started over four decades ago in response to a challenge issued by the United States' space program: create a handheld light that could simulate the intensity of sunlight. By creating a million candlepower handheld light, a group of engineers succeeded and went on to form Streamlight.

Streamlight and Panasonic have a long history together. When Bob Villari, Panasonic Senior Account Manager, assumed responsibility for the Energy Sales division's business with Streamlight, he immediately focused on developing a deep understanding of the company's market pressures, business objectives, and competitive challenges. Villari forged value-focused relationships with buyers, engineers, and executives across Streamlight's organization and aligned them with Panasonic's resources, gaining trust and respect at all levels.

Through multiple collaborations between the parties, Villari recognized that Streamlight's vision for the future aligned well with Panasonic's direction, and he sought to expand the value Panasonic could provide. He brought key people from both organizations together for face-to-face collaboration, a significant investment for both parties and a testament to their trust-based relationship. Participants included Streamlight's president, head of engineering, and head of purchasing, and from Panasonic, the executive liaison between Japan and the U.S., the lead engineer, and the head of manufacturing operations from their China-based factory. As a result of the meeting, Streamlight decided to move a significant piece of business from another provider to Panasonic, and a foundation for new value-added business to follow was established.

Tony Hehn, Group Manager of Panasonic Energy Sales Division, puts it this way:

> "Driven by a relationship-based sales process, Bob Villari connected the dots between our organizations and gained Streamlight's trust and respect at all levels, right up to the president. We aligned ourselves with their organization from engineering to the factory, and were able to help them define their needs. This created value for both of us and opened doors to new opportunities."

The Impact: Why Engagement Excellence Matters to Panasonic's Customers

To help manufacturers around the world build world-class products, Panasonic engages with customers to provide engineering expertise throughout the product development process. By investing time up front to understand what their customers are trying to accomplish and where they have challenges, Panasonic is better able to position their resources, capabilities, and products throughout the engagement to co-create value for their customers' customers.

Through their collaborative partnership Streamlight and Panasonic are able to generate better lighting solutions and identify new, innovative opportunity areas of development. When customers like Streamlight choose to embed Panasonic technology in their products, they demonstrate strong confidence in Panasonic's ability to deliver on their own brand promise of performance, quality, and reliability. Ray Sharrah, President and CEO of Streamlight, observes:

> "At Streamlight, we're committed to providing quality products, timely delivery, and comprehensive training to our customers who depend on us for their portable lighting equipment. We achieve this through the expertise and dedication of our people and our partners, who stand behind this commitment. Our partnership with Panasonic is a good example. They know our business and work side-by-side with our engineers to design outstanding technology into our products. They also work with our factories to ensure production flow, especially when we need to meet unexpected demand from our customers. Whether its technology, manufacturing, or distribution challenges, we trust the Panasonic team and know we can rely on them to get it done."

The Takeaway: Why This Matters to You

As the partnership between Panasonic and Streamlight demonstrates, engagement excellence begins long before there is an opportunity on the table. Listening with an open mind, Panasonic gains deep knowledge of their customers' businesses, both in terms of how their products are used and in the challenges they face, and then helps customers grow their businesses in ways that benefit everyone: Panasonic, their customer, and their customer's customers.

This depth of understanding serves as the foundation for every collaborative partnership, and has been especially valuable to Panasonic's design-in opportunities with Streamlight. Having earned Streamlight's deep trust across their organization, Villari brought both companies to the table. With resources aligned, the Panasonic team was able to position and differentiate their value, which resulted in a significant win for both parties, as well as opportunities to expand their partnership. Villari describes it this way:

> "Through collaboration between our teams, mutual innovation, and value co-creation, we both won. Panasonic was able to offer an improved solution that, in turn, enabled Streamlight to better satisfy their customers' needs, establishing a strong foundation for a long-term partnership between our organizations. When your efforts to create value with your customer result in value creation for their customers, everybody wins."

Panasonic believes that excellent customer engagement is central to their commitment to quality. Through collaborative customer engagement, the company is able to harness the power of innovative technologies, engineering and manufacturing expertise, and global resources to build long-term partnerships and provide added value before, during, and long after the sale.

III

Grow: Driving Success After the Sale

STRATEGY 9

Realize the Value: Meeting and Exceeding Customer Expectations

YOU ACCOMPLISHED a lot in Sections I and II, but your work is far from finished. In the four strategies we discuss in Section III, you'll learn how to extend your customer engagement into a strong, lasting relationship that will endure and grow after the sale and beyond.

In Section I, pre-opportunity and well before the sale, you made a commitment to engage differently. Through research and diligence, you became a student of your customer, learning as much as you could about their business and what's going on in their world. Noting your interest and preparation, the customer welcomed your invitation to explore possibilities together, and through that process, your knowledge evolved into an understanding of what matters most to them.

With no tangible opportunity yet in sight, you persevered, investing still more time and effort. Together, you and your customer visioned their success. You helped them identify areas of future potential value and prioritize those things that might be achievable. Finally, based on everything you learned, you identified customer value targets and elevated the conversation with your customer because you understood what they needed, how you could help, and why it mattered to them. Pre-opportunity became a very real, newly-minted sales opportunity.

In Section II, you proceeded with confidence into the sale. You entered this phase of customer engagement proactively, not waiting for an RFP to land. Energized and committed, you came prepared to deepen your knowledge of your customer's business—to discover their external drivers, business objectives, internal challenges, and even their success criteria. By asking the right questions and focusing on your customer, you were able to transform your insights about what's important to them into actionable awareness that could be implemented on their behalf. Your actionable awareness enabled you to align effectively with your customer's team, and in the process, build a network of sponsors and supporters for you and your organization.

Your authenticity and credibility earned you the right to position the fit of your solutions, and you built a unique value proposition and customer-specific message for this opportunity. As your customer continued to realize that your engagement with them was different—more focused on their needs than on your products—you captured customer mindshare, which allowed you to effectively position your fit and deploy the strategies that would drive your plan to win.

Differentiating your strengths, you demonstrated how your unique value would enable your customer to meet their business objectives, as well as how your solutions would allow them to resolve their challenges. By focusing on the things that matter most to them, you captured their preference, and as a result, your customer concluded that you and your organization could deliver superior value versus that of your competitors. Not surprisingly, you won the opportunity and your customer awarded their business to you.

You've arrived at this point, ready to pursue success after the sale, for some very specific reasons—namely, the first eight of our twelve strategies for a customer-driven world. But before we turn our attention to the next four strategies, let's pause for a moment of introspection and reflect on the following questions:

- **If you hadn't engaged differently, would you be where you are with your customer?** Your customer undoubtedly noticed a difference in how you engaged with them. Do you have evidence that they engaged differently with you as a result, both before and during the sale? If you believe you would have won their business anyway, do you think you would have won at the same price points and terms?

- **If you were to identify the primary reasons that you won your customer's business—drawing from your research, exploration, visioning, and elevation in Section I, and your discovery, alignment, positioning, and differentiation in Section II—which reasons would you put first and second?** If we asked your customer's team members why they selected and awarded their business to you and your organization, how do you think they would answer? If we asked them what set you and your team apart from other suppliers that pursued this business, what do you believe they would say?

- **In your application of Strategies 1 through 8, can you identify the specific inflection points that propelled your momentum, accelerated your execution, or significantly advanced your customer's willingness to collaborate with you?** Were there times during the sale when internal engagement within your own organization felt more challenging than your external engagement with your customer? Are you able to project how you could apply *Engage/Win/Grow* strategies to your colleagues and internal customers?

What Happens After the Sale?

If you want to effectively navigate how your relationship with your customer evolves after the sale, you'll need a few more strategies to deploy. But first, you have to make a decision: Will you plan to grow with your customer, or will you hit the pause button, kick back, and celebrate your recent win?

Readers with the heart of a hunter may wonder why furthering the relationship with this customer is better than turning their attention to new business opportunities. We understand this mindset, and we see it all the time. Hunters track and kill their prey, eat it, and get back out in the woods as soon as possible so they can do it again. Not a bad approach—as long as there's plenty of game to be pursued. But consider this: as a customer, would you want to be thought of as prey to be flushed out and hunted? Or would you prefer to build a relationship with a supplier that wants to grow together with you, adapt to your needs, participate in realizing the promises made before the sale, be accountable for your success, and stick around for the long haul? Those in the latter category are sometimes referred to as *farmers*, *gatherers*, or *growers*, because they want to ensure that the value they promised to their customers is realized, and that expectations are not just met, but exceeded. We hope this choice—if you have a choice—will be a simple one for you. Most salespeople and account managers believe that there is an advantage to maintaining and growing a customer relationship rather than replacing it with another, and we do, too.

You planned to engage, and you were effective. You planned to win, and you were successful. Now, you'll be planning to grow, building on your relationship with your customer by meeting and exceeding their expectations, and driving your success into new opportunities. When you move beyond the sales process and employ all twelve *Engage/Win/Grow* strategies with your customer, you'll find that what follows after your last sale is likely to be your next opportunity.

Delivering on Promises and Expectations

From the time you began to explore possibilities with your customer to the point where you created a preference for your solutions and value, your customer has been experiencing the difference in how you engage. They like and appreciate the way that you focus on them. At some point, they may have wondered, "What will happen after the contract is signed?" Customers almost never want their salesperson to go away after the sale. If they hadn't felt that you have brought value to the relationship, they probably would have bought from someone else. Bernard Quancard, the CEO of SAMA, offers this perspective:

"We're witnessing a dramatic change in both the buying habits and value expectations of today's customers, yet too many suppliers cling to the sales styles and approaches of the past. Tomorrow's winners will be those suppliers that engage differently and help their customers realize the value that was promised during the sale. We see this in our community of practice at SAMA: in the end, a supplier's growth will be determined by the success of their customers."

When customers start talking about how things changed after a sale, what follows is rarely an endorsement of their supplier. Think of it this way: if you become part of your organization's value based on how you engage, and then you vanish when the sale is over, from your customer's perspective, some of your organization's value disappears with you, along with the knowledge, insights, and actionable awareness that you brought to the table.

As Your Stress Level Drops, Your Customer's Rises. Inevitably, as soon as the ink dries on the contract (and sometimes before), your customer's attention will shift to what you already know is most important to them: their success. Don't believe it? Then ask yourself when you last heard a customer, post-purchase, suggest going back and discussing price and renegotiating the terms of the contract they signed with you last week, last month, last quarter, or last year? It almost never happens, because the customer has to focus on getting things done. The external drivers, business objectives, and internal challenges you discovered in Strategy 5 are still in play, and they matter to your customer now more than ever.

Thanks to your hard work in creating and articulating an expectation of future potential value, your customer's team members have become more accountable to their organization for realizing that value, and you and your organization have been entrusted to help. Now that they've entered into an agreement with you to deliver, their need to overcome challenges and achieve objectives is more palpable throughout their organization, and their expectation that you will be on hand to create the value you've promised has become more imperative. For your customer, there couldn't be a less opportune moment for you to disappear.

In their evolution from buyer to owner, your customer's reality has shifted; the pressure is mounting, they are worried, and their stress level is rising. If you pull a vanishing act now, when they need you most, you will create a relational void and a continuity gap that will be difficult, if not impossible, to overcome later. What happens after the last sale will have serious repercussions on your next one with this customer, if there is ever to be another.

Your organization may be one of many that deploy a shared system of customer-driven responsibilities. This approach works well in a variety of B2B selling environments, especially when internal alignment is strong. But all too often, after the sale, another scenario tends to unfold:

1. The sale ends.

2. The contract is signed.

3. A transition, or hand-off, takes place.

4. The salesperson moves on and doesn't make another appearance (unless there is another opportunity).

5. A new contact is assigned to the account (who lacks the credibility, trust, knowledge, information, insights, actionable awareness, and relationship earned and exhibited by the original salesperson).

6. The customer is less comfortable with that new contact, and the relationship's energy levels drop.

7. The customer feels worried and stressed (as well as abandoned, disappointed, and angry).

The Problem with Sales-in-a-Vacuum. *Engage/Win/Grow* includes three phases for a reason. If the sole purpose of your engagement is making the sale, then an "engage/win/disappear" model would have sufficed, and this book would have ended with Strategy 8. But this sales-in-a-vacuum mind-set (which unfortunately does exist) ultimately results in unhappy, disenchanted, and dissatisfied customers with no reason to be loyal to their supplier. You and your organization can avoid this mentality and devolving into vendor status; how you do it is up to you.

To ensure the growth of their strategic or key customers, some companies deploy strategic account management processes and best practices; it's a solid approach, at least for the relatively few customers that are considered strategic (generally less than 2 percent, typically less than 5 percent, and always less than 10 percent of the total customer population). But what if you're a supplier that simply can't make the commitment to strategic account management? What can you do to avoid being perceived as selling in a vacuum?

After the sale, you earn the right to tap into a vast and powerful asset that too few suppliers discuss with their customers or even acknowledge that they have. Past proven value is a living testimonial to the success that you, your organization, and your customer have had together. It's simple and powerful, and, perhaps best of all, it's free (because you've already invested in and committed to it).

Every time you meet and exceed your customer's expectations and they realize value as a result, you make deposits into an ever-growing and expanding pool of assets, the "accounts" that constitute your past proven value. You've earned these deposits through your hard work with your customer, and they are a powerful statement of mutual success that grows each time you and your customer experience value creation and co-creation together. Unless you have underperformed with your customer, past proven value always favors the incumbent, which is you, before your next sale to that customer.

Yesterday's Future Potential Value Is Tomorrow's Past Proven Value

In Section I, you did your homework and pondered possibilities for future engagement with your customer, which led you directly into visioning exercises that allowed you and your customer to identify areas of future potential value. This collaborative vision of your customer's success was so compelling that both of you agreed to formalize the discussion into clearly defined customer value targets and make a mutual commitment to pursue those of highest priority. This was the basis for the opportunity that you just worked on and won.

Throughout Section II, you focused on the things that mattered most to your customer: their external drivers, business objectives, and internal challenges. You worked hard to discover and validate this information. You were deliberate in aligning your team internally and then your team members with your customer's as you sought to align your objectives with theirs. You positioned the fit of your solutions against your customer's challenges, and you differentiated the uniqueness of your value to enable your customer to meet and exceed their objectives and requirements. Finally, you demonstrated the connections by combining the insights and actionable awareness you had developed into a concise value framework that showed your customer how your solutions would help them overcome their obstacles and resolve their problems, and ultimately, how you would deliver value that would help them achieve success.

Ask yourself an important question: Are there clear connections among the future potential value and value targets from *before the sale*, the differentiated value that created customer preference *during the sale,* and the past proven value that will be memorialized *after the sale*? The answer is absolutely yes. Your commitment to these three dimensions of customer value will continue to separate you from competitors who are only interested in hit-and-run selling. When customers tell us that there is something different about how certain salespeople and account managers engage with them, this is what they're referring to, and it's easy to see why they like it; turning the promise of future potential value into the reality of past proven value means that your customer has achieved success. And you are part of that achievement.

Memorializing Your Commitments to the Customer. The customer-specific value upon which you based your proposal to the customer in Strategy 8 was the basis for the sale that you just won. Now it's time to make your proposed value real. Your customer is relying on you to meet their expectations and deliver the success you visioned and committed to together. What once was only a possibility has evolved into an opportunity, which in turn has evolved into a commitment that you and your organization have made to your customer. The customer-specific value proposition that helped you engage differently before and during the sale will now help you and your team engage differently after the sale.

Think of your customer-specific value proposition as a covenant with your customer, an articulation of the value you propose to bring through the fulfillment of your commitment. You've promised to provide solutions in the form of your products, resources, expertise, services, customer experience, and brand/reputation, and now it's time to make good on your pledge. Your customer must have liked your approach or they wouldn't have selected you, so don't abandon it now. Your value proposition provides an excellent framework for documenting your value creation and co-creation efforts, as well as a means to memorialize your customer's successful experience with you over the entirety of your relationship.

What you do after the sale is vital to your future aspirations with your customer because it's where proposal promises become value realities, which is the main thing that customers expect whenever they buy. As you continue to create and co-create customer value together, your organization's willingness and ability to go the distance with your customer whenever they give you the opportunity to do so becomes indisputable. Pity the salesperson who fails to stick around for the realization of value with the customer, because this is where the *real* celebration occurs and where enduring relationships are forged that will provide momentum before each future sale.

Past proven value is the asset that grows each time you win a new opportunity and move on to create and co-create value with your customer. It is a repository for all the customer-specific value that has been created so far, and you can continue to grow it over time simply by keeping your commitments to your customer. Past proven value is just as compelling for your customer. It provides them with an ongoing value summary that preserves and updates a record of the successes that they have experienced with you, and the value that you have created and co-created together. Your past proven value also provides a foundation for periodic updates and reviews with your customer, as well as the content and format for in-the-moment discussions of value that can be important when you're working with customers over an extended period of time.

The Components of Past Proven Value. Past proven value is determined by tallying up and summarizing the external drivers, business objectives, and internal challenges that you and your organization helped your customer address in the past, as well as the solutions you have provided and the unique value that you've created and co-created together (Figure 9-1).

After the sale, past proven value represents an aggregation of your history with the customer and a record of your previous value creation efforts. It highlights what mattered most to your customer at specific points in time, and provides a composite way to look at your success with the customer.

In Strategy 5, we developed the concepts of customer external drivers, business objectives, and internal challenges, and extended them to include your solutions and value in Strategies 6 through 8. When you define your past proven value, you repurpose these concepts to reuse in a different tense and with a different dimensional view. What was happening then has now happened, and the living picture you are creating becomes richer and

DETERMINING YOUR PAST PROVEN VALUE

MOST RECENT OPPORTUNITY		EARLIER OPPORTUNITY		EVEN EARLIER OPPORTUNITY		YOUR PAST PROVEN VALUE ACCOUNTS
Past Drivers	+	Past Drivers	+	Past Drivers	=	Customer's External Drivers Addressed
Past Objectives	+	Past Objectives	+	Past Objectives	=	Customer's Business Objectives Achieved
Past Challenges	+	Past Challenges	+	Past Challenges	=	Customer's Internal Challenges Resolved
Solutions Provided	+	Solutions Provided	+	Solutions Provided	=	Your Solutions Provided
Value Realized	+	Value Realized	+	Value Realized	=	Value Created and Co-Created

Figure 9-1. Determining your past proven value.

more compelling. Each success provides you with deposits into these past proven value accounts:

- **Your customer's past external drivers.** Starting with your most recent opportunity and success with your customer and working back in time, what external drivers, pressures, and market factors (including the customer's competition, customers, and shareholders, as well as such factors as the economy, government, and technology) have impacted your customer and motivated them to take action? (If this is your first success with your customer, your past proven value will include only this opportunity.)

- **Your customer's past business objectives.** Reflecting on your most recent opportunity and success with your customer and working in reverse order of occurrence, what business objectives and plans has your customer put in place (including efforts to increase revenues, decrease costs, or reduce business risks) to address their external drivers, pressures, and market factors?

- **Your customer's past internal challenges.** Thinking again about your most recent opportunity and working in reverse order, what internal challenges and potential blocking factors (obstacles, hurdles, problems, and other issues) could have prevented your customer from achieving their business objectives and plans?

- **Your solutions provided.** What solutions (products, resources, expertise, services, customer experience, and brand/reputation) have you delivered to your customer in the past and how have your offerings enabled them to resolve their challenges and achieve their objectives? Be specific and use the six components listed in your description of the solution (see Figure 7-1); these details enhance your credibility and the impact of your message.

- **Your value created and co-created.** How have you created and co-created value through the solution components that you have delivered, and how has this value helped your customer achieve their business objectives and address their external drivers? How is your value unique, and how does it connect directly with those objectives and drivers?

If you're planning to grow with your customer, there's no better place to start than with the success that they have experienced with you and your organization, and with the past proven value that you have created and co-created together. Additionally, you can gain significant momentum when you leverage your past successes with the customer, and there is hardly a more powerful means for entering your next opportunity than with the wind at your back from the success of your most recent sale. Sure, there's still work to do before you begin to focus on your next sale. You will need to ensure that you validate your value creation results with the customer (Strategy 10), adapt and change the approach as needed to meet their evolving needs (Strategy 11), and expand and grow your customer relationship to new levels (Strategy 12). But with the deposits that you're making into your past proven value accounts, you're certain to be looking at new opportunities ahead; it's just a matter of time.

Value Realization, Consolidation, and Articulation

There's no time like the present to begin capturing your past proven value, because as your customer is realizing value through their relationship with you and your organization, you're ideally situated to make direct deposits into all five of your past proven value accounts (Figure 9-1). Once your summary of past proven value has been started, keeping it current is relatively easy, and your customer may even participate in updates, providing you with ideal opportunities for ongoing value collaboration.

New levels of actionable awareness can develop as you capture your customer's external drivers, business objectives and internal challenges, combine your insights into a composite view, and look at the dynamics of your customer's business over time and across multiple opportunities. When you consolidate the value that has resulted from your prior successes with your customer, an interesting picture emerges. Some salespeople and account managers are too focused and singular in their view of the opportunity at hand, pleased that it has developed, and ready to build their plan to win. A true student of the customer, however, will pause to consider how the customer's past external drivers, past business objectives, and past internal challenges connect with those of the present (and those that will be discovered in the future). It makes for an interesting perspective on the long-term trends of your customer's business.

When you help your customer realize the value they expect, consolidate it into a summary, and articulate it throughout their organization (including with their senior management and procurement organizations), you enable them to tell a compelling story of mutual value creation. This powerful message will pay dividends to both buyer and seller over the long haul due to your continuing success with your customer and the ongoing deposits you will make into your past proven value accounts going forward (Figure 9-2).

SUMMARIZING YOUR PAST PROVEN VALUE

Customer's Past External Drivers:
What external drivers, pressures, and market factors have impacted your customer and motivated them to take action?

Customer's Past Business Objectives:
What business objectives and plans did your customer put into place to address their external drivers, pressures, and market factors?

Customer's Past Internal Challenges:
What internal challenges and potential blocking factors could have prevented your customer from achieving their business objectives and plans?

Your Solutions Provided:
What solutions have you delivered in the past and how have they enabled your customer to resolve their internal challenges and address their business objectives?

Value Created and Co-Created:
How have you created and co-created value that has helped your customer achieve their business objectives and address their external drivers? How is your value unique?

Figure 9-2. **Summarizing your past proven value.**

When you discuss past proven value with your customer, don't be surprised if they ask for a summary. When they do, we encourage you to share it with them. After all, it's a snapshot of success that features your customer and you, and there's a much greater likelihood that you'll have more opportunities for value creation if you're able to share the results of your past proven value with the members of the customer's team.

Testing Your Effectiveness: Realize the Value

The following six sets of questions will help you determine the effectiveness of your value realization with your customer:

1. **As you consider the value that you and your organization are creating and co-creating with your customer after the sale, how much can be traced back to your early engagement with them before the sale?** Does that value include insights you gained through your research? Does it include possibilities you explored early on with your customer?

2. **Can you identify a pre-opportunity engagement point at which you and your customer discussed future potential value together?** If so, did your discussion include visioning what success might look like to the customer's team members? Did it result in the identification of customer value targets that you agreed to pursue?

3. **During the sale, you collaborated and created a customer-specific value proposition with your customer that was based on what mattered most to them, and you helped them understand how you and your organization could contribute.** To what extent did your value proposition evolve as you engaged in more focused discovery with your customer? Did your in-depth discovery support you in aligning with your customer in the areas most important to them? How would you describe the key areas of actionable awareness that developed through your discovery efforts with your customer? What types of actions were

taken by you and your team in response to these emerging areas of awareness?

4. **When you compare the solutions and value that you and your organization have committed to create and co-create with your customer after the sale to where you started when you were before the sale, what has changed?** As your opportunity evolved during the sale, did your value proposition, messaging, and conversations evolve as well? Where are the inflection points at which your mindshare with the customer expanded, and their preference for you and your organization seemed to escalate?

5. **As you work with your customer after the sale, have your discussions included any of the customer- and opportunity-specific information that you are now capturing in your summary of past proven value?** Are any new and different drivers and pressures impacting their business, and if so, what are they? How have their business objectives changed? Are their challenges and potential blocking factors largely unchanged, or have new problems and obstacles arisen after the sale? If it's the latter, how would you describe them?

6. **When you consider the deposits that you are making into your past proven value accounts after the sale, are you able to clearly articulate how the solutions that you have provided (and are providing) connect with your customer's internal challenges and business objectives?** What are the connections between the value that you are creating and co-creating and your customer's business objectives and external drivers? Can you articulate them clearly? Does your customer understand these connections? If so, could their team members articulate the connections to others within their organization?

STRATEGY 10

Validate the Impact: Measuring Success with Your Customer

HOW DID YOU FEEL when your customer told you that they had decided to move forward with you and your organization? Few events in the life of a salesperson or account manager are more exciting and euphoric than the moment of winning. At the instant your customer declares that you have captured their preference and they want to partner with you, only you know the distance you've already traveled, and how difficult and stressful the journey was at times. If not for your diligence, discipline, and tenacity, you would likely have ended in a very different place.

Along the road to your win, you may have encountered managers who suggested that you were investing too much time into this customer, and that you should cut your losses and move on. But you refused to heed their warning—a good decision, because now you are in the process of helping that customer achieve their vision. You went the distance, won the trophy, and can turn your attention to ensuring that you and your organization both meet and exceed your customer's expectations, as well as help them realize the value that you promised.

On its surface, the way forward may seem direct, but there are some perplexing questions to face: What does success really mean? Who will determine if the results are adequate? What criteria will be used to reach a conclusion? Did you and your organization keep your promises, meet your commitments, provide the solutions, create the value, and deliver the results that your customer expected?

If you feel your elation begin to evaporate, we completely understand. In sales and account management, joy is fleeting. Just as you're sitting back, basking in the warmth and radiance of your new sale, and contemplating the deposits being made into your past proven value accounts, your customer is having a different kind of experience. Their team members are starting to feel nervous because they just made a significant and potentially unsettling transition from the protective cocoon of a buyer to the accountability of a full-fledged owner, and now you have to ensure that your organization measures up to your customer's expectations.

Until now, your customer has worked hard to keep their buying process and evaluation on track. They may have had to caution their vendors not to go charging around the decision team and into their company's executive suite. They may have received some not-so-good news about their business last quarter, which could mean the budget for your project has been reduced—they're going to have to do more with less. Or they might have been notified by their procurement organization that the rules have been revised, so they're concerned that you will not accept their newly implemented 90-day payment terms.

Just when your customer needs you more than ever, a growing number of forces and factors could undermine their relationship with you. They sense things spiraling out of control and feel powerless to prevent the deterioration of something that felt great to them just a few short weeks ago. The decisions and choices they've made are about to bear fruit—or not. Things have gotten serious. Now your customer has to deliver.

Measuring Success with Performance Impact Zones

If you're ever going to get another business opportunity with this customer, a number of the right things have to happen after the sale. In an ideal world, you and your customer will have agreed on what those things are during the sale. If you did, then you've earned a hearty congratulations. If you didn't, you may find that what you won is not what you had anticipated, based on what is now expected of you and your organization.

Performance can be measured in more ways than we have time to review here, and there's something good to be said about most methods. But with all the talk about big data, data analytics, business intelligence, and CRM management reports, the problem that some organizations bring on themselves is trying to measure too much. If you and your customer attempt to assess everything, it's likely that you won't measure much of anything, because you won't be able to focus on the things that really matter.

Rather than getting bogged down, we can suggest a simple approach to success measurement and results validation, and it should be relatively painless to implement with your customer. You and your organization have customer expectations to meet, and there's no time to implement new systems or rework old processes. It's *after the sale* and the clock is ticking; you have to start assessing the value you are helping your customer realize by measuring results.

Consider it inevitable that your customer will subject your organization to post-sale performance measurement, and you may have heard rumblings that assessment is imminent. But the pendulum swings both ways. How has your customer performed? Are you prepared to measure? If you've ever had a customer that was so difficult you wondered whether you wanted to continue doing business together, you know it's not a good feeling—no matter what the outcome is.

We've asked our clients' customers what they consider to be important in their relationships with their vendors, suppliers, and partners. Their responses tend to differ based on the level of their relationship with a supplier and how the parties engage to do business together (see Figure 6-2), but most customers' expectations after the sale aggregate into four distinct performance measurement categories or "impact zones"—*value, alignment, relationships,* and *growth,* as Figure 10-1 shows. In Strategy 11, you'll learn how these zones can be applied from your perspective, but for now, let's think like your customer.

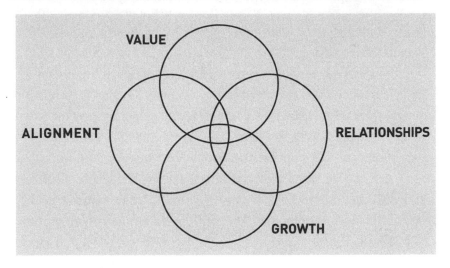

Figure 10-1. **Defining the impact zones of performance measurement.**

Value can be interpreted differently from relationship to relationship—for example, a customer that you consider to be strategic as compared to a customer that purchases transactionally and considers you a vendor. Every customer will have a value expectation. In Sections I and II, we developed the topic of value extensively, because many consider it to be the ultimate measure of success in business. Previous strategies have looked at value in terms of how customers define it, and how you deliver it. You won your customer's business and this opportunity because your customer-specific value proposition (not your product proposition, resource proposition, expertise proposition, or services proposition) differentiated you from your competitors. You proposed to do something that has value to your customer, and now it's time to deliver.

Alignment can be defined in terms of making connections that include people, resources, solutions, best practices, cultures, and business objectives. When a customer and supplier are in operational alignment, business tends to happen on time, on budget, and according to plan. When customer and supplier are aligned team-to-team, doing business can seem easier, more productive, and less frustrating because everyone spends less time figuring out how to navigate the other organization. Customers and suppliers that are aligned tend to do business more effectively, efficiently, and less stressfully than those that aren't.

Relationships can extend beyond business-to-business alignment to a more personal level. We've never heard a customer say that their relationship with their salesperson or account manager was unimportant, just as we've never heard a customer claim that they wanted to be controlled, processed, hunted, or taken captive during the sale. Not once. And while there are theories floating around on the Internet about the death of relationships in B2B sales, as well as the extinction of B2B salespeople, we simply disagree. Relationships are and will continue to be important, and they start with you.

Finally, *growth* can mean very different things to different companies and people, and because you effectively engaged before and during the sale, you don't have to guess what it means to your customer. Their growth will depend on their ability to address their external drivers by putting achievable business objectives in place, and you already know what those are. After the sale, it's your job to ensure that the unique, differentiable value that you promised will actually help your customer meet and exceed their objectives and reach the goals that you visioned together.

Growth refers to more than just top-line revenue. Your customer might also include improving their competitive position in a market, doing business more profitably, and acquiring an increasing amount of industry knowledge and best practices—all things that you can potentially impact. Your customer's realization of value (as reflected in your summary of past proven value) is predicated upon you and your organization delivering on the visions and promises you proposed.

Your legacy with your customer is about to be determined. It's time to get serious about turning possibilities, visions, propositions, and proposals into realities, and ensuring that your customer is successful as a result of their engagement with you. To do this, you will need to understand how these results will be measured and validated.

Benchmarking Performance from the Customer's Perspective

Customers appreciate knowing that you expect to be accountable for their success after the sale is complete; it provides them with a sense of reduced risk. It's especially reassuring when you, the individual they've worked with from the beginning, are as committed to meeting and exceeding their expectations now as you were to developing the opportunity and making the sale previously. We don't say "closing" the sale because if you're going to remain engaged after the sale happens, then you are, in fact, *opening* something. You've engaged, you've won, and now that it's time to grow, you'll be opening up a whole new set of possibilities to explore and successes to vision.

Let's begin by reviewing where you are with your customer:

- **What your customer plans to do.** After engaging in discussion and capturing the external drivers and market factors putting pressure on your customer's business, you discovered the business objectives to address them that your customer put in place.

- **Why they need your help.** As you went deeper into discovery with the members of your customer's team, you developed an understanding of the potential internal challenges, obstacles, and blocking factors that could prevent the successful execution of their objectives.

- **How you proposed to help.** Based on what you learned, you aligned your products, resources, expertise, and services with your customer's internal challenges and requirements, and proposed a solution that you and your organization could deliver.

- **Where you differed from the alternatives (why your customer selected you).** As you demonstrated to your customer how your solutions and value would enable them to resolve their internal challenges and achieve their business objectives, they recognized a difference between you and your competitors. This uniqueness, reinforced by the work you did before and during the sale, convinced them that you and your organization were the right choice.

Figure 10-2 provides a set of customer impact factors—those areas of your performance most critical to your customer—as examples for you to consider. As you review the list, keep in mind that it is highly unusual for a customer to ask for your commitment to and accountability for all of them. It can happen, but a set of customer expectations this broad and deep should be connected with a very large sale!

As we discuss these factors, think about your last sale of magnitude and see if you can identify at least one item in each impact zone that might

BENCHMARKING PERFORMANCE: YOUR CUSTOMER'S PERSPECTIVE

IMPACT ZONE	CUSTOMER IMPACT FACTORS
VALUE	Delivery of your products, resources, and services per terms of our agreement
	Access to your subject matter and industry experts for consultation with us as needed
	Prompt resolution of problems and conflicts as they arise
ALIGNMENT	Fit of your solutions, products, and services against our business needs and requirements
	Connections between our teams to ensure ease of doing business
	Synchronization of your business processes with ours for greater efficiency and productivity
RELATIONSHIPS	Development of executive-level relationships among our senior management and yours
	Assignment of dedicated resources to support our account and understand our business
	Commitment to manage our account strategically and not just transactionally when we are buying from you
GROWTH	Opportunities to grow our revenues by expanding our product portfolio through co-innovation
	Opportunities to increase our margins by reducing our costs of doing business through collaboration
	Opportunities to become more efficient using your solutions through sharing of best practices

Figure 10-2. Benchmarking performance from your customer's perspective: examples.

describe your customer's expectations. If you're selling commodities, some of these zones may apply less, because when a decision is based purely on price and contract terms, it is less likely that you would have developed the type of customer-specific value proposition and created the types of value expectations that are reflected in these examples.

Don't get too hung up on whether an impact factor belongs in one particular zone or another. The zones and factors connect and overlap. So as you consider the following examples, keep in mind that they intersect because they represent what matters most to your customer, and the things that matter most to your customer are interconnected.

Value. Every zone is about *value* at one level or another, but to ensure more granularity and actionable awareness, the categories of value considered here are those that we discussed in Strategy 8: your products, resources, expertise, services, customer experience, and brand/reputation.

- **Delivery of your products, resources, and services, per the terms of your agreement with the customer.** Meeting contract terms is typically among the most visible and binary examples of value. If you can't make good on your agreement, there are sure to be problems ahead. *Have you delivered, are you delivering, and will you continue to deliver to your customer what has been committed to— on time and on budget?*

- **Access to your subject matter and industry experts for consultation as needed.** Product superiority is becoming more and more difficult to maintain. When your customer sees value in the expert resources you can provide, they're telling you that they value consultation, and the knowledge and insights you can transfer to them. *Do you have access to resources that can transfer knowledge, expertise, and insights, and have you made them available to your customer?*

- **Prompt resolution of problems and conflicts as they arise.** Customers are like the rest of us: they don't like to wait and they don't like to worry about their problems escalating. When your customer values prompt, proactive customer service, they're inviting you to perform at a level that will increase their speed of business and decrease their stress levels. *Have you briefed your customer service team on your customer's expectations of prompt, proactive problem resolution? Do they clearly understand how the proposed services they must now deliver will help your customer resolve internal challenges and achieve their business objectives?*

Alignment. When you think of alignment, consider the types of connections that may be important to your customer. In Strategy 6, we discussed the alignment of people, resources, solutions, best practices, cultures, and business objectives, among others.

- **The fit of your solutions, products, and services against the customer's business needs and requirements.** Delivery is important, but as your customer begins to use and implement your solutions, products, and services, they will look for fit and alignment with their needs and requirements. They may suggest that you focus on operational performance in such areas as quality, accuracy, and completeness. Based on their perspective, you will need to decide not just what you will do, but also how you will do it. *Given your knowledge of the customer and what your organization will deliver, are you confident that you will align with your customer's expectations regarding fit, quality, accuracy, and design?*

- **The connections between the two teams ensure ease of doing business.** Team-to-team alignment requires effort, but the payoff in terms of stress reduction for you and your customer can be significant. When your customer values integrated teamwork, they're typically looking for ways to align organizations and minimize the time they spend navigating your company to get the things they need. *Have you made the connections between your customer's team members and yours? Is this alignment understood by everyone? If a serious issue with navigation develops, does your customer know who to contact for resolution? Is that go-to person you?*

- **Synchronization of your business processes with the customer's for greater efficiency and productivity.** When your customer sees value in aligning your processes with theirs, they are typically interested in efficiency, productivity, and consistency. You should do everything possible to ensure that you get off on the right foot after the sale with a customer that has this type of value expectation. *Have you done your part to align your processes with your customer's, and do the people within your organization who are responsible for executing (accounting, customer service, etc.) understand what is expected of them?*

Relationships. Relationships matter to customers, perhaps more today than ever before. Customers also care about who from your organization they will work with, and how you will approach and manage your relationship with them.

- **Development of executive-level relationships between the customer's senior management and yours.** Relationships are more important than ever in B2B commerce, and the customer that values senior-level relationships is interested in exchanging access to the executive suite with you. Relationships with these customers tend to be collaborative, and described as "partnership" and "trust-based." *Have you suggested a meeting between your customer's executives and yours? If so, have you developed an agenda, shared it with your customer, and briefed your executives on your objectives for the meeting?*

- **Assignment of dedicated resources to support the customer's account and to understand their business.** Most customers are interested in having resources that will work with them after the sale, but some *really* care, and they place a premium on the people who will engage with them. For these customers, there is significant value in working with people who know their business and, once the relationship is established, they don't like to change. *How will you determine the optimal resources for your customer? How* *will you ensure that your team members understand your customer's business and what's expected of you and your organization?*

- **Commitment to manage the customer's account strategically and not just transactionally when the customer buys from you.** Even providers of commodity products implement strategic account management programs; it's a way to differentiate themselves. The customer that values a strategic relationship with you has probably been a strategic customer before, so it's a good idea to find out what value they received as a result of their strategic relationship with another partner or supplier. *Do you and your organization engage in account management and planning with your strategic and key customers? If so, how will you involve your customer in these efforts? If not, when do you plan to start?*

Growth. About much more than just the numbers, growth can take on a variety of different meanings to your customer. When you discuss growth with your customer, consider asking them to describe the types of growth that are needed to support their objectives and challenges (such as knowledge, best practices, skills, market position, and quality).

- **Opportunities to grow the customer's revenues by expanding their product portfolio through co-innovation with you.** Customers that value innovation and co-innovation look for growth via the new ideas you can bring to help them develop new products, create value for their customers, and gain competitive advantage. Their relationships with suppliers that can innovate and co-innovate typically result in value co-creation and partnerships. *Have you discussed possibilities for innovation and co-innovation with your customer? If not, when do you plan to do so? Does your organization have a history of this type of engagement with customers? Are there internal resources available to help you get started?*

- **Opportunities to increase the customer's margins by reducing their costs of doing business through collaboration with you.**

These customers want you to help them get more value from what they currently spend. They want to do business more cost-effectively, which can translate into exploring new possibilities and visioning new successes with you. They are looking for growth that is related to margins and the bottom line, and if you help them do business more efficiently and at lower costs, you become well-positioned for future opportunities. *Can you find ways to give your customer more value from their existing spend with you by doing business more cost-effectively? If you were to help them achieve this, how would it impact your future business?*

- **Opportunities to become more efficient using your solutions through the sharing of best practices.** Customers that value knowledge, skill, and best practices are likely to become effective and efficient users of the solutions and products that you provide. They place a premium on doing things right and will invest in training their people and ensuring that they stay up-to-date on new product releases. They are typically interested in how you can help them increase or accelerate their growth in product, industry, and technical knowledge. *Have you helped your customer understand your company's training and knowledge transfer capabilities? Is the customer a candidate for any best practice sharing forums that your organization provides?*

Intersection Points Among the Four Impact Zones. By now you've noted the intersection points and interconnectivity among the four impact zones, and you've given some thought to how you will validate your impact and measure your customer's success by seeing things through their eyes. As you peer through this lens, remember the importance of your past proven value: the impact you are having on your customer's world through the results you provide to their business is being directly deposited into these accounts. And, as we are about to see in Strategies 11 and 12, your investments are about to yield exciting returns as you deliver on your promises of customer success and continue to gain momentum after the sale.

Testing Your Effectiveness: Validate the Impact

The following six sets of questions will help you determine your effectiveness at validating your impact with your customer:

1. **As you consider the evolution of your customer's needs in terms of their business objectives and plans, did you observe changes as you transitioned from** *before* **to** *during* **the sale?** Is there clarity among the members of your team regarding what your customer is planning to do and why they need to do it?

2. **Have the internal challenges and obstacles that you discovered and discussed with your customer during the sale remained constant, or are there any "moving targets" to be considered?** Do your team members have clarity regarding the severity of your customer's challenges and obstacles? Are they aware of potential roadblocks that may be encountered in resolving them?

3. **Are there any areas of your customer-specific value proposition (and the proposal and agreement to proceed that were based on it) that give you pause to reconsider your ability to meet your customer's requirements?** Are you and your team members on the same page regarding the depth and breadth of your customer's expectations, as well as the ability of your solutions, products, expertise, resources, and services to meet and exceed them?

4. **Having demonstrated your unique value to your customer in ways that help them distinguish you from other alternatives, how would you prioritize your specific areas of value differentiation in terms of importance to your customer?** Are there "main things" that your customer is expecting in terms of your results, value creation, and impact? If so, how would you suggest that the customer measure and validate them?

5. **With respect to the value-related impact factors that you identified, have you determined how you will measure and validate**

your performance, and communicate what you learn with your customer? Have you determined how you will measure and validate alignment-related impact factors with your customer?

6. **With respect to the impact factors associated with relationships, have you determined how you will measure and validate your performance and communicate this with your customer?** Have you determined how you will measure and validate growth-related impact factors with your customer?

STRATEGY 11

Adapt the Approach: Applying Lessons Learned with Your Customer

THINK ABOUT the lessons life has taught you. Did you learn more from your successes or from the things that didn't go as well as you had expected? If you're like most people, you've gained something from both kinds of experiences, but the most powerful and profound learning often occurs on those occasions when a do-over would have been nice, but wasn't possible. When disappointment and understanding collide, the emotional impact can be difficult, but it's these kinds of circumstances that teach us the most.

As a sales or account management professional, you ride an emotional roller coaster every day. You go from high to low and back, based on the success of your efforts to engage effectively (both internally and externally), win repeatedly (sometimes in difficult situations without the full support of your organization), and grow consistently (in your relationships with customers and your colleagues). Then, just when you feel that you're figuring it all out, when your confidence is growing, and you're about to kick into high gear, everything changes, you lose momentum, and you're forced to hit reset.

Change is inevitable in sales and account management. How you respond to it will have a significant impact on your success, because sales and account management are about customers, and customers operate in a continual state of rapid change, especially in today's business environment. Not adapting is simply not an option. Unless you want to be left behind, it's never too soon to begin planning for the inevitable changes that will become part of your future with your customer. It's time to prepare yourself to learn with your customer and adapt as their needs evolve.

Your customer has undoubtedly had ups and downs with their suppliers, and after the sale, they're starting to think about the type of relationship they will develop with you over time. At the moment, things are feeling pretty good, and that's because of how you've engaged with them up to this point. Now that you're delivering on their expectations, they've started realizing value and they may even be doing some validation and measurement. But they still wonder what their relationship with you will be like once the glow of success has faded from your recent sale and another customer starts absorbing your time and attention.

Your customer is about to make a *decision after the decision.* They are going to decide where you fit into their supplier paradigm. Are you a vendor, someone they do business with because it's convenient, or are you a preferred supplier, someone who is important to their business? Are you a planning partner who has become necessary to your customer, or have you been elevated to trusted advisor, essential to their business success? As they consider your relationship, they're going to focus on lessons learned and your ability to adapt going forward.

A senior executive once said something to Steve that offers insight on your customer's perspective. Steve had met with this executive to discuss how his client and the executive's organizations could work together more effectively, more collaboratively, and more strategically going forward. The executive, pleasantly surprised at the topic, remarked, "When we're planning, executing, and reviewing, I'm spending money. My best chance to *make* money is when it's time to adapt and change, yet this is precisely when all of my vendors disappear!"

As a result of the approach illustrated in Figure 11-1, you and your customer entered into a new level of relationship based on a willingness and commitment by both organizations to engage in the following:

1. Heightened levels of collaboration; you *plan* together.

2. Mutual action plans that both parties would be accountable to *execute.*

3. A periodic *review* of the plan's progress and measurement of mutual success.

4. Discussions of lessons learned; *adapt* approaches and update plans.

Things might have turned out differently had there not been a level of transparency that facilitated this kind of conversation. You earned that transparency by engaging differently with the customer than your competition did, and the result was an elevated relationship between the parties.

What kind of supplier does your customer perceive you to be? If you want your relationship to evolve beyond that of a vendor or preferred supplier to planning partner or even trusted advisor, there's no time like the

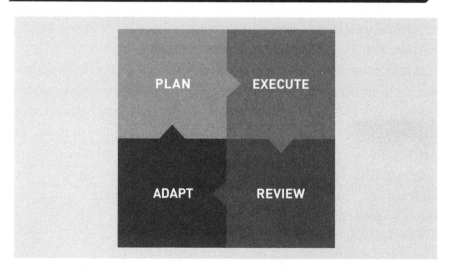

> PLANNING TO GROW WITH YOUR CUSTOMER AFTER THE SALE

PLAN   EXECUTE

ADAPT   REVIEW

Figure 11-1. Planning to grow with your customer after the sale.

present to start the planning process with your customer. And the best place to begin is in the *Adapt* quadrant of Figure 11-1, where you look for ways to improve performance together. Will you be required to invest yet more time and resources to make this happen? Absolutely, but you're going to do it anyway; it's just a question of whether you'll make that investment in a new, possibly unknown prospect or in your recently-satisfied customer. Not sure what to do? Here's a hint: conventional wisdom says it's typically easier and cheaper to keep a customer than to get a new one, and your authors agree.

Understanding How Your Customer Defines Success After the Sale

Long before the sale, you visioned success with your customer, visualized future potential value together, and defined value targets that you committed to pursue with them. Much has happened since then, so the question now becomes how your customer's needs and requirements have evolved, shifted, or transformed from those value visions *before the sale* and value proposals *during the sale*. There's a strong likelihood that something has changed, even if you responded to documented requirements in an RFP, because continual change is the nature of business. And the best time to adapt your approach and adjust your course with your customer is now, because it only becomes more difficult later.

If you're planning a future with your customer, you start by understanding how the value they expect is being realized (Strategy 9) and by validating the impact that you and your organization are having on their business (Strategy 10). These are the leading indicators that you will need to embrace if you're going to be in a position to proactively plan with your customer. You may be inclined to relate this way of thinking with account planning, and indeed it is. But the logic is driven by three activities that are consequences of your last planning effort with the customer:

1. **Execution.** *During the sale* you planned to win, which constitutes your most recent collaborative effort with your customer. If you

both feel that both organizations are executing effectively, then it speaks well of the success that your customer is experiencing as a result. Execution after the sale is about implementing Strategy 9 and helping your customer realize the value that you promised and committed to them. *Are you meeting your customer's expectations through the value that they are realizing after the sale? Are you exceeding their expectations?*

2. **Review.** In your most recent review of the progress-to-date with your customer, how did they assess your performance against their expectations and milestones? If they feel that you are delivering the business outcomes they anticipate, then it's likely that you're measuring up and performing well against the customer impact factors defined in Strategy 10. *When you and your customer review and evaluate outcomes, are you performing to their expectations? How do they measure your impact on their success?*

3. **Adaptation.** Here in Strategy 11, we will address your willingness and ability to adapt and change based on the results of your execution and review. Things may be going so well since you concluded the sale that nothing needs to be changed or even adjusted. It's not impossible, but it is unlikely, and over the longer term with customers, it rarely turns out to be the case. They are going to experience change, and either you will adapt your approach to enable your organization to grow with them, or you will find yourself out of alignment, and ultimately, out of favor. *As a result of your execution and review of results-to-date, how can you apply the lessons learned, and where do you and your organization need to adapt your approach?*

Your customer's perspective on success will determine where you go after the sale, as well as how you get there. Salespeople and account managers who plan collaboratively with their customers, execute and deliver results, subject themselves to review, and embrace a willingness to adapt and change will be better positioned for future success. And while this seems logical and reasonable on the surface, the reality of today's selling environment is that many more salespeople don't engage this way than do. After the sale, it won't take long for your customer's team members to determine what your approach is, and they'll be watching for clues on how your relationship with them has changed from what they experienced before and during the sale. They've been through it with other suppliers, and they're hoping that your engagement with them after the sale will continue to be effective. And they know that they're about to find out.

Adapting Your Approach to Meet Your Customer's Changing Needs

You and your organization are about to show your customer the true colors of your business impact, as measured by performance benchmarking in Strategy 10, and as categorized into the four impact zones: *value, alignment, relationships,* and *growth.* The good news is you don't need much new information at this point, because you've already established what success looks like to your customer, the value they expect to realize in their pursuit of that success, and how you will measure and validate your performance against their expectations and realizations.

You gained this awareness by understanding what mattered most to your customer before the sale and then by discovering as much as you could to develop the insights and actionable awareness required to engage effectively during the sale. You made deliberate connections with your customer as you proceeded, aligning your team members with theirs and positioning the fit of your solutions against their requirements. You then advanced your opportunity by building and implementing the right strategy for positioning yourself to differentiate how your value would best enable your customer to meet and exceed their objectives.

As your customer started to realize the value that you had promised to create and co-create with them, you began to capture and summarize it as past proven value, and you developed a performance benchmark for you and your customer to use for validating your impact on their business. In Strategy 11, you're looking at where you are with your customer, and you're deciding what course corrections are necessary to ensure that you will be able to expand your relationship with them in Strategy 12.

Embracing Change and Making Needed Adjustments

Change is difficult for salespeople. We know because we're salespeople ourselves, and throughout our careers we've watched salespeople resist the new and unfamiliar. The evidence is clear. If salespeople and account managers were more open to change, we would adopt proven sales enablement technologies more readily than we do, and we would stop resisting and ignoring the compelling evidence that they can increase sales productivity. Whether a next sale is to follow your last one will be determined, to a large extent, by your willingness and ability to embrace change on behalf of your customer.

The sample customer impact factors in Figure 10-2 help you identify and focus on specific areas where change and flexibility on your part will enable you to expand and grow your relationship with your customer. To illustrate, we have identified one item from each impact zone to serve as an example of how you can assess the extent to which you and your organization can and will embrace potential change. As you apply these examples to your customer, think about how you will adapt your approach to provide the business impact that they expect.

- **Value: Prompt resolution of problems and conflicts as they arise.** If your customer continues to tell you that it's taking too long to get problems resolved and that they have to talk with too many people to reach final resolution, you know there's a need for change.
  Adapt your approach: When your customer is frustrated and believes something is lacking in terms of your organization's problem resolution, can you adjust or streamline your process for resolving customer problems to provide faster response times by either adding additional resources or eliminating steps?

- **Alignment: Connections between your team and theirs ensure ease of doing business and navigation of your organization.** When your customer's team members are confused about how they should be engaging with your company's resources to get things done and feel they're wasting time trying to find their way around your organization, there's a need for change. If your customer finds that you're not easy to do business with, the situation is only going to get worse if nothing changes.

  Adapt your approach: How can you ensure that the mapping and alignment of your organization's resources to your customer's is optimal? What measures can you put in place to clarify and simplify these connections for your customer?

- **Relationships: Your commitment to manage the relationship strategically and not just transactionally when the customer is buying from you.** When customers think you're too focused on the next sale and not focused enough on their strategic future with you, there's a need for change. Customers don't like to feel that relationships with their most important suppliers are out of balance, and when they do, it's almost always because they feel that your short-term priorities are taking precedence over what they consider to be the bigger picture and their longer-term needs. You can feel good about this one, because you won't hear it from a customer unless they want a long-term relationship with you.

  Adapt your approach: How can you become more strategic in your engagement with your customer? Can you introduce account management and planning best practices into your relationship?

- **Growth: Opportunities to grow revenues by expanding their product portfolio through co-innovation with you.** When your customer expresses disappointment in the levels of collaboration, innovation, and co-innovation they have with you and your organization, there's a need for change. Opportunities to brainstorm, co-innovate, and co-create are a privilege (and typically put you on a direct path to planning partner), so you should value being asked to participate in these types of discussions. You won't be asked unless the customer recognizes the knowledge, expertise, and creativity that you can bring to the relationship.

Adapt your approach: How has your organization engaged in these types of activities with other customers in the past? How can you apply these experiences and supporting resources to the growth expectations of your customer? Do you have access to the internal resources required to adapt, co-innovate, and co-create value with them?

We've looked at adaptation and the need to change from your customer's perspective, but what about yours? You and your organization should have the opportunity to weigh in on the direction of the relationship and how you plan to grow it. In strategic customer relationships, there's typically an authenticity and trust level that ensures that neither party will look for success at the expense of the other, and no one is grabbing for the last dollar. Both parties understand that as value is realized, success is validated, and approaches are adapted for future growth, something special happens in the relationship that can yield significant returns to everyone over the long term. But to get to that type of relationship, you have to focus your attention on what matters most to you and your organization as well, and to find a way to align your definition of success with how your customer defines it. Let's examine the impact of this customer relationship on your business, and assess performance in terms of what's most important to you.

Validating the Impact on Your Business to Ensure Both Parties Are Successful

A successful relationship between two organizations engaged in B2B commerce requires that the parties relate to each other effectively. This may seem obvious, but it is precisely where problems seem to develop. Experience repeatedly shows that when a seller relates differently to a buyer than the buyer relates to the seller, the relationship is likely to be characterized by a lack of alignment and harmony, and tends to become unbalanced.

Don't assume that this only happens when your customer thinks less of you than you think of them. This pendulum swings in both directions; "the customer is always right" simply won't suffice if your intent is to develop and grow an effective long-term partnership.

We're not about to deviate from the customer-first perspective we've taken throughout the book, but when *customer first* devolves into *customer only* and the relationship begins to slide in the direction of win/lose (with you as the loser), you run the risk of breaking your *Engage/Win/Grow* circle. Sometimes early warning indicators tell you that it might be coming: a notice from procurement that all providers are now under mandatory 90- or 120-day payment terms is a good example. When the 2008 recession began, many organizations felt compelled to hold onto their cash for as long as possible, so some organizations issued this requirement to their entire supplier community. If you were in a vendor relationship when you received this letter, then you probably weren't surprised. But if notification arrived and you had developed a more successful relationship with your customer, perhaps even a partnership, then it most likely didn't feel good to you or your organization. You may have even taken it personally.

Another example of a customer request that is difficult, if not impossible, for most suppliers to meet is *most-favored-nation* (MFN) pricing, which means your customer is receiving the best price you have ever offered for comparable goods and services. At its heart, this concept has merit in its attempt to prevent discriminatory pricing of products. But your product is only one of the six components of value that we introduced earlier, so applying MFN to organizations that are not selling commodities and have a broad, deep value proposition to offer is an effort to devalue and commoditize the things that are, in many cases, the most important to your customer.

Also, MFN pricing requires you to agree that if you ever sell at a lower price, your customer will receive remuneration for what they overpaid. Imagine your customer's shock and disbelief if you attempted to turn this around—if, sometime in the future, they pay someone else more for what they once bought from you for less, and therefore are obliged to send additional payment to compensate you, the underpaid supplier. The point is this: if you and your customer are going to extend and expand your relationship, there should be enough transparency for you to let them know when you need some help with something, and at least be able to discuss it reasonably.

Benchmarking Performance from the Seller's Perspective

In Strategy 12, we'll discuss how to proactively grow and expand your customer relationship by leveraging the value that your customer has realized and the deposits you've made into your past proven value accounts. But before you can do this, you'll have to take stock of where things stand with your customer today, and determine how you will need to adapt your approach to ensure that you'll be well positioned to grow and partner with them in the future. How strategic would you like to become to this customer? If you haven't been thinking about this, it's time to start.

In Strategy 10, we considered your customer's perspective on your performance as a supplier—and now you'll think about the performance that you and your organization need to experience based on your investment in this customer relationship. You're going to leverage the same lenses or impact zones, adjusting them to focus on performance from *your* perspective. If you're going to extend your efforts to engage effectively, win new business, and grow your relationship with your customer, you'll need a plan.

You'll begin by considering an alternate set of examples that focuses on what's important to you and your organization going forward. Thus far, after the sale, you've primarily focused on ensuring that your customer is realizing value and on track to achieve success by meeting and exceeding their objectives. You've also taken steps to identify areas of potential improvement that will enable you and your organization to grow with them.

We suggested that your customer is wondering how their relationship with you will develop; aren't you wondering the same thing? If we can agree that no salesperson or account manager should be satisfied to remain in a vendor relationship with their customer forever, then let's conclude that you should, at the very least, strive to be a preferred supplier, and evolve the relationship over time to planning partner or beyond (wherever possible). The examples provided in Figure 11-2 are typical of the impact factors today that are shaping customer relationships from the supplier's perspective—yours.

As we go through the list, reflect on a recent sale that includes examples of your impact factors at work. As we suggested in Strategy 10, it's less important which factors go into what zones than which examples apply to your customer. And keep in mind that these zones—*value, alignment, relationships,* and *growth*—represent the four most important words in

BENCHMARKING PERFORMANCE: YOUR PERSPECTIVE		
IMPACT ZONE	**YOUR IMPACT FACTORS**	**FOCUS AREAS FOR GROWTH (& WHY?)**
VALUE	Share of customer's spend in your markets	Y N
	Opportunity to collaborate, innovate, and co-create with your customer	Y N
	Opportunity to share best practices with your customer	Y N
ALIGNMENT	Fit of your solutions, products, resources, and services with your customer's needs	Y N
	Your competitive position with your customer (mindshare and preference)	Y N
	Alignment of your engagement processes with your customer's buying and decision processes	Y N
RELATIONSHIPS	Your customer's willingness to partner with you and your organization	Y N
	Your customer's consideration of you and your organization as strategic to their business	Y N
	Customer sponsors and supporters for you and your organization	Y N
GROWTH	Number of your customer's subsidiaries and business units doing business with you	Y N
	Opportunities to grow revenues with your customer	Y N
	Opportunities to do business more profitably with your customer	Y N

Figure 11-2. Benchmarking performance from your perspective: examples.

contemporary strategic account management. They will also be important in the plan to grow that you are going to build with your customer.

Value. When you consider value as an impact factor for you and your organization, think about how you define it.

- **Share of the customer's spend in your markets.** You're likely to focus here and seek change if your customer is doing significantly more business with some of your competitors than they are with you. This is more an opportunity than a problem: if the other guys have this business locked up, how were you able to win the opportunity you just won?

- **Opportunity to collaborate, innovate, and co-create with your customer.** You're likely to adapt your approach in this area if you believe that by engaging in more collaboration, innovation, and co-creation with your customer, you'll be able to explore new possibilities, visualize future potential value, and pursue new customer value targets.

- **Opportunity to share insights and best practices with your customer.** If you believe that demonstrating thought leadership by sharing insights and best practices with your customer can open new doors, then this is likely to be an area of focus and adjustment for you.

Alignment. Your alignment impact factors are those areas where your connections with your customer will be improved as a result of your proactive planning.

- **Fit of your solutions, products, resources, and services with your customer's needs.** Customers decide all the time to purchase solutions that are not the best fit at prices that are not the lowest. If this situation applies to you, how will you and your organization adapt going forward?

- **Your competitive position with your customer (mindshare and preference).** You'll be inclined to focus on this area if you believe that, despite your recent win, you are still not where you want to be in terms of competitive position among the customer's other options and where your customer places you going forward, with respect to their other options for the markets you serve. You should focus here if you intend to plan for improvement, which will translate into greater customer mindshare and specific areas where they clearly prefer you and your organization.

- **Alignment of your engagement processes with your customer's buying and decision processes.** Almost everyone's stated objective is to do business with the customer the way the customer wants to do business, but that's much easier said than done. Focus here if it's clear that your processes are out of sync with your customer's, because it's only a matter of time before these types of issues become exacerbated.

Relationships. Your relationship with your customer and their team members can affect your ability to optimize future performance together.

- **Your customer's willingness to partner with you and your organization.** Focusing here does not necessarily mean that your customer is *unwilling* to partner, but more likely an indication that pursuing mutual goals and objectives has plenty of upside for you. Be advised: in any giving market, customers tend to enter into only one or two true partnering relationships.

- **Your customer's consideration of you and your organization as strategic to their business.** When this is not the case, some organizations respond with a primary call-to-action regarding the investment of their resources and deployment of strategies for growth. If you choose to focus here, you and your organization should also be prepared to consider your customer as strategic to *your* business, which is not necessarily a given.

- **Customer sponsors and supporters for you and your organization.** Focus here if you believe that your future growth can be assisted by members of your customer's team who sponsor and support you today (see Strategy 6), or that your growth will be inhibited if you don't expand this important network.

Growth. It's practically a given that revenues will be on this list, but there are other important factors to consider that can serve as leading indicators of revenue growth. The first item below is a good example of this.

- **The number of your customer's subsidiaries and business units doing business with you.** Everyone understands that you're far better off to have your business spread across your customer's organization than to be in only one or two of their subsidiaries or business units, yet salespeople and account managers repeatedly put themselves at risk by doing so. You may choose this as an area of focus, and decide to keep it selected.

- **Opportunities to grow revenues with your customer.** Now that you've engaged, won, and are preparing to chart a course for growth with your customer, you'll want to focus here if you believe that your future with the customer is ripe with additional business opportunities, whether you can identify them today or not.

- **Opportunities to do business more profitably with your customer.** Your organization may feel that the cost of doing business with your customer is unacceptable, or, more specifically, that the price points at which you are doing business can't be sustained. Focus here if you have work to do regarding margins and developing a more profitable relationship with your customer.

Adapting Your Approach and Planning to Grow

As you worked through the impact factors, you may have noticed potential connections between those that you identified as important to your customer in Strategy 10, and those that you selected here as areas of future focus. If you see connections, then consider it a bonus. Either way, you now have enough information, insights, and actionable awareness to begin your planning to grow efforts and expand your relationship with your customer.

Expanding the relationship with a customer means different things to different people, and there are a variety of ways to assess relationship expansion, starting with the impact zones that we've been discussing. But for most people in sales and account management; when it comes to the question "What now?" there's one answer that is more enticing than any other: "The next sale." It's precisely why we're going to end with the beginning in mind. In Strategy 12, you will see how to leverage the work you've done to make the critical connection: *after* your last sale to *before* your next one.

Testing Your Effectiveness: Adapt the Approach

The following six sets of questions will help you determine your effectiveness at adapting your approach with your customer:

1. **As you reflect on your history of planning to grow with your other customers after the sale (plan, execute, review, adapt), which areas are your strengths?** *Which areas need improvement going forward? If we asked your customers to rate your effectiveness in each of these four areas based on recent history with you, what would they say?*

2. **If we asked your customer's team members to describe the value that they have realized thus far after the sale, how would they respond?** *If your customer's team members were asked to validate the impact of their decision to do business with you, what would you expect to hear them say? If your customer has experienced disappointment in one of these areas (plan, execute, review, adapt), which would it be and why?*

3. **Have you learned any significant lessons to date that would suggest course corrections or adapting your approach with your customer?** *If so, what are they? How would you organize your course corrections and adaptations into the impact zones (value, alignment, relationships, and growth)? How would you prioritize them?*

4. **If we asked your customer's team members whether they have learned any significant lessons that would suggest course corrections or that you adapt your approach, what would they say?** *What would they suggest as course corrections and adaptations? How do their suggestions organize into the four impact zones? How would they prioritize them?*

5. **Based on what's most important to you and your organization going forward, how confident are you that both you and your customer are able to realize your objectives?** *What are the potential opportunities to connect your priorities with your customer's?*

6. **What is the one "main thing" that needs to happen going forward in order to meet and exceed your customer's expectations of you?** *Do you believe that you can increase your likelihood of being where you would like to be with your customer one year from now by engaging with them collaboratively and developing a proactive plan to grow your relationship together?*

STRATEGY 12

Expand the Relationship: Leveraging Your Past Proven Value

THUS FAR we've discussed eleven proven strategies for the customer-driven world we live in today. Now we turn to the final one, Strategy 12, and it is the key to determining whether your implementation of *Engage/Win/Grow* will be a circle or a straight, flat line. In Strategy 12, you will determine what your future with your customer will look like, and what type of relationship you, your organization, and your customer will forge together.

Don't think for a moment that your customer will determine whether your relationship is about to expand; they won't. They may hold the big vote regarding certain specifics, and that's the way it should be. But when you trace back almost any B2B relationship that is considered a partnership between organizations, you're likely to find that the supplier, led by an engaged salesperson or account manager, took the initiative and made the investments to evolve the relationship to the next level. They accomplished this by proving that it worked to the customer's advantage as well. SAMA CEO Bernard Quancard observes:

> "The greatest legacy of the customer/supplier relationship is the value that has been created and co-created between the two organizations,

and yet so many sellers miss the opportunity to celebrate this success with their customers. The fulfilled promise of value for each completed sales opportunity provides fuel for building and expanding the relationship like nothing else can. If you want to grow your business, just do everything possible to help your customer achieve success, and then watch: the results will be amazing!"

Responsibility for the direction your relationship with your customer takes rests largely with you, and it's time to decide how you will move forward together.

You and Your Momentum: In Motion and Growing Stronger

You've got something going for you now that should be a factor as you consider the future with your customer: momentum. A direct result of the hard work, resources, and time that you've invested, momentum may be intangible, but it can have a dramatic effect on your future. It's no accident—you made it happen by applying the proven strategies of *Engage/Win/Grow* and thinking far beyond the traditional sales process. Before your customer was buying, and before there was a specific opportunity in sight, you made it your business to become a student of your customer's business. You researched their organization, and based on what you learned, you took action.

You could have waited, like others did, for your customer to come to you, but you didn't. You initiated a dialogue to find out what your customer cares about. You leveraged what you learned and began to inquire, making a conscious decision to invest more of your time. Your customer agreed to explore possibilities with you because they realized that you weren't trying to sell them anything; you were asking questions and demonstrating a sincere interest in their business and where it was going. Your refreshing approach wasn't lost on your customer. They liked that you were engaging with them differently than the salespeople and account managers they worked with from other companies.

It seemed almost natural to extend your discussions into what your customer was trying to do—to vision success together and consider how you could help them achieve it. Not surprisingly, you were able to elevate the conversation from its focus on what your customer cared about to the things that mattered most to them. You and your customer defined value targets, which they agreed to pursue with you. As they did so, they continued to feel that there was something different about you and how you engaged with them. The value targets that you defined together were compelling to your customer, and so was your approach. The time you invested before the sale had yielded quite a return, and your momentum propelled you forward, with an exciting opportunity now in hand.

As you probed more deeply to discover the external drivers, business objectives, and internal challenges motivating your customer to take action, you learned more about their success criteria, you aligned your team with the customer's team, and your relationships became stronger. As your credibility grew, so did their trust in you and your organization, and as you engaged vertically and horizontally within their organization, you developed sponsors and supporters, and deepened your understanding of their business. Your knowledge and insights evolved into actionable awareness, which guided you and your team to take the right actions at the right times.

Knowing your customer had choices, you continued to engage differently, positioning the fit of your solutions and developing a value proposition for the opportunity that was specific to your customer and its team members. Your solution addressed the things that mattered most to them, and you showed them how your products, resources, expertise, services, customer experience, and brand/reputation connected with their specific wants, needs, and requirements. As your competitive position grew stronger, your mindshare with your customer expanded. The time to execute your plan to win and differentiate yourself from their other choices had arrived.

As you demonstrated the uniqueness of your offerings and differentiated your value to your customer's decision team, you sensed the gap widening between you and the competition, and that your customer's preference for you and your organization was growing. You articulated your customer-specific value message clearly, concisely, and compellingly, and when you learned that the customer had selected you and your organization, you gained momentum again, this time in the form of a new sale. Your time during the sale was well spent, and you moved forward with your customer and your commitment to create and co-create value.

Momentum is an appropriate description of what happened as you executed Strategies 1 through 8. Your momentum before and during the sale made you stronger as you entered the *after the sale* phase. Now you and your team are working to help your customer realize the value that you promised to deliver and ensure that their expectations are met, and even exceeded. You're supporting these efforts by measuring performance, tracking success, and validating the impact that your organization is having on your customer's business. And, you're adapting your approach and making the necessary course corrections to ensure that your customer experiences the value, alignment, relationships, and growth that are important to them. You're building past proven value, and it looks like you and your organization will soon be celebrating a significant success with your customer. You've accrued momentum yet again through your execution of Strategies 9 through 11, bringing you to where you are today.

The momentum you feel as you enter Strategy 12 is compelling, because it obliges you to answer two important questions about yourself and your organization:

1. Will you keep moving forward with your customer, or will you begin to lose focus and momentum?

2. Have you been strengthened by your success thus far, or will your efforts with your customer begin to diminish and recede?

An invaluable asset to salespeople and account managers, momentum can serve as the conduit between what you've done and what you will do. But you have to seize momentum when it's available if you are to receive the benefits, and you're precisely where you need to be to do so.

Something significant is about to happen between you and your customer, and how it plays out has everything to do with how you harness the energy of your momentum and plan to grow a successful future together. It's by no means a foregone conclusion that your implementation of *engage* and *win* will be followed by *grow*. There are other approaches: some go with "engage/win," which suggests they're simply going about their business elsewhere after the sale, as will their customer. Somewhat more optimistically, a few opt for "engage/win/wait," which involves lengthy periods of anxiety-ridden downtime and repeatedly checking for the next RFP to be issued. Then there's "engage/win/procrastinate," which means you know what you should be doing after your last sale, but have some very credible excuses for not doing it. And finally, there's "engage/win/get replaced."

You've probably seen salespeople and account managers execute each one of these four alternative processes, and maybe you have too, on occasion. But that's all behind you. Will you fight the wind at your back and lose the momentum you gained from your work in Strategies 1 through 11 by not taking action? Of course not. You're breaking new ground with your customer: you engaged, you won, and now you're growing.

Your plan to engage in Section I was effective, and the energy you created before the sale helped you accelerate into Section II. Your plan to win was successful, and the momentum from your sale propelled you into Section III. Now, it's time to go beyond the sales process and ensure that your *Engage/Win/Grow* circle remains unbroken by leveraging your past proven value, planning to grow with your customer, and expanding your relationship with the customer.

Building Your Plan to Grow with Your Customer

When you think about building a plan to grow with your B2B customer, there are typically four core questions to consider:

1. How have you helped your customer realize value?

2. Who achieved success as a result of this value?

3. Why should your customer re-engage with you?

4. Where could you help your customer achieve success again?

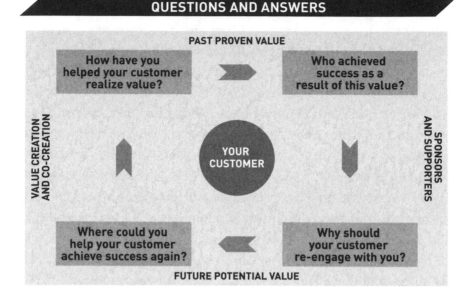

Figure 12-1. Expanding your customer relationship: questions and answers.

If you're going build an effective plan to grow with your customer, your responses to these four questions can provide the parameters for doing so. Figure 12-1 provides the context and also suggests a logical output as you consider expanding your relationship.

Looking at a plan to grow your customer relationship in terms of these four questions can simplify the notion of account planning and growth strategy into something concise and easy to apply. As we unpack each question, think about your customer and how the plan to grow that you are building will expand your relationship with them.

Question 1: How Have You Helped Your Customer Realize Value? This is the question to start with if you're growing your relationship with an existing customer. Past performance is a reasonable predictor of future performance, and most people believe that the second time around with a supplier won't be any better than the first. Question 1 has a distinctive ring of the past tense, because your value is not conjectured, imagined, hypothesized, or simply promised; it has happened and it is proven.

Customers often retain their memories of *past painful disappointment* much longer than those of past proven value, but don't blame them—it's human nature, and the very reason that it's important to maintain an ongoing summary of your successes with your customer. An incumbent provider that has delivered value typically has an advantage over a newcomer, because in B2B commerce it's generally assumed that when you've effectively delivered value to a customer, it is likely that you will again. When you consider question 1, it should be in the context of what your past proven value means to your customer. It summarizes the realized value you have delivered that enabled your customer to address their external drivers, achieve their business objectives, resolve their internal challenges, and meet their success criteria.

Question 1 begins with "How" because the power of past proven value is in demonstrating *how* the things that matter most to your customer connect to the things that matter most to you. When you show your customer how you can help them by connecting the components of your solutions (your products, resources, expertise, services, customer experience, and brand/reputation) directly with their challenges, and the uniqueness of your value with their objectives, you make a powerful and enduring statement that memorializes value and success for both parties.

Question 2: Who Achieved Success as a Result of This Value? Some customers relate to your past proven value on a personal level, because they remember quite clearly the pressures of their external drivers, the intensity of their business objectives, and the stress of their internal challenges. Think about your personal experiences: When someone helps you with a pressure, plan, or problem, doesn't your memory reflect favorably on that individual? Of course it does, and your customer is no different. It's important to check in with the members of your customer's team you considered to be your sponsors and supporters during the sale (and even some that you didn't), to perform a kind of process check and perhaps even to do a bit of homework to see where things stand.

After the sale your customer is wondering how your relationship might change going forward. At this point, your efforts to develop relationships at all levels of your customer's organization come back into consideration. There's no doubt it took time to build these high-impact relationships, and more time to grow them, but our experience conducting win/loss analyses clearly shows that the existence (or lack thereof) of an executive-level sponsor is likely to influence decisions that are made and outcomes throughout the customer organization. When you arrive at question 2, you'll find that the success that your customer sponsors and supporters have achieved provides you with additional momentum for growing your relationships with them.

You'll find a tool on this book's website—BeyondTheSalesProcess.com— that provides a comprehensive version of the relationship assessment we discussed in Strategy 6 and summarized in Figure 6-2. Applying this tool to your sponsors and supporters can be an interesting way to assess your relationships at the individual level, as well as the organizational level. It can also be applied to any member of your customer's team, whether they are your sponsors and supporters or your competitors. Sponsors and supporters almost never view you and your organization as just a vendor, because they typically consider you to be at least important to their business, and perhaps even necessary or essential. And it's likely that they don't have the same high regard for certain of your competitors.

To expand your customer relationship, you have to consider the people involved and try to see things from their point of view. Their success as a result of the value you created and co-created with them will be a significant factor in your growth plans. As your customer relationship expands, make it a priority to grow your customer network by developing new sponsors and supporters.

Question 3: Why Should Your Customer Re-Engage with You? Early on, we discussed the importance of providing your customer with a reason to engage, and the need to continue doing this after the sale is just as important. Even if your relationship with your customer is outstanding, an evil element in the world of B2B commerce runs wild and poses a relentless threat to keeping you and your organization "top of mind" for your customer. "Too much information" and its close companion "too much data" can make it difficult for you, your team members, and your customer to identify what's important from a bottomless reservoir of irrelevant hype and noise available online. And it's only going to get worse.

Giving your customer another reason to engage matters because of mindshare, which we discussed in Strategy 7 in terms of your positioning strategy, and expanded upon in Strategy 8 in the form of preference. Your customer has a lot to think about these days, and the easier you can make it for them to keep you in mind, the better off you'll be. Your response to question 3 will result from combining the outputs from both questions 1 and 2, and considering them together. "Why should your customer re-engage with you?" is almost certainly answered with a combination of your past proven value and the customer sponsors and supporters with whom you created and co-created it.

Your customer now has history with you, and it's been positive. You've proven in the past that you can create value, and that value has impacted the personal success of specific individuals. Sticking with the incumbent supplier (or at least giving you a strong shot at the business) is a straightforward and logical decision for most customers, if the value you provided helped them achieve success.

Another way to look at question 3 is to ask, Why *wouldn't* your customer want to re-engage with you? You've gone the distance and created value in the past. This is precisely why question 3 is about what your customer believes that you can do for them in the future, otherwise known as your future potential value. Your customer will find it much more difficult to believe that you have the potential to offer future value if you haven't delivered in the past, which is all the more reason that past proven value is an asset that pays dividends for the salespeople and account managers that use it.

Question 4: Where Could You Help Your Customer Achieve Success Again? Question 4 closes the loop on your plan to grow; it takes your answers from the previous three questions and asks what every customer wants to know: if you delivered once, can I trust you to deliver again? There are few guarantees in B2B commerce and past proven value is not a promise of future perfect performance. But the likelihood of success should be at least as great in the future as it was in the past. If that's the case, and if, as the incumbent, you have the relationships and track record, why wouldn't you be in a strong position as a result?

There is an important difference between questions 3 and 4. Question 3 asks why your customer should re-engage with you. Question 4 asks where you can help your customer achieve success again; it's all about the specific places where you can create value going forward. To answer the question, you'll need the benefit of insight and actionable awareness—not a problem for you because of the value you've created and the relationships that you've developed. Of course, you can always learn more, and as a student of your customer, you're well advised to continue your quest for knowledge about their business, and avail yourself of learning opportunities that arise. The distinct advantage to being an incumbent under consideration for future business is that you've done the research, exploration, visioning, and discovery with your customer, and as a result, you've gained alignment, customer mindshare, and preference.

You will ultimately find more places to create and co-create additional value and help your customer be successful again in the next round of customer value targets that you will define collaboratively together. Your opportunity for future business may be as close as your next conversation with your customer about the external drivers and pressures that are impacting their business, the business objectives and plans that have been put in place to address them, and the internal challenges or obstacles that are threatening their success. Put another way, you will determine where you will create new value by borrowing from Strategy 4 and identifying what your customer needs to do, how you can help, and why it matters, both to them and to you.

Ending with the Beginning in Mind

As we've discussed building a plan to grow and expanding your customer relationship, you may have noticed certain concepts and terminology from previous strategies creeping into the discussion. You may even have recognized some specific references to *Before the Sale* concepts discussed in Section I. If you're feeling concerned that we are being redundant and maybe even careless with our terminology, then you'll be pleased and reassured to learn that we've done it with purpose. Figure 12-2 shows why.

Figure 12-2 adds depth to Figure 12-1, which should make it clear that when you plan to grow and expand your customer relationship, you'll find yourself ending with the beginning in mind. Discussing your past proven value with your sponsors and supporters provides an ideal opportunity to further your customer research and add to your knowledge of their business at a time when the conversation is all about their success with you and your organization (Strategy 1). When your discussions with sponsors and supporters evolve into identifying specific reasons for re-engaging with you, it's a great time to explore the possibilities, brainstorm what the future has in store for them, and identify the things that they care most about (Strategy 2).

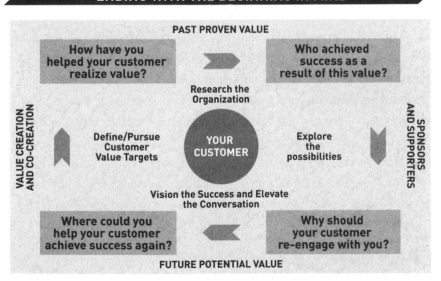

Figure 12-2. Expanding your customer relationship: ending with the beginning in mind.

As your customer re-engages with you and provides you with guidance about the types of value that they must deliver to their organization, you're in an interesting environment for visioning future success together (Strategy 3), and as you do so, elevating your conversation and defining new value targets that you and your customer will ultimately agree to pursue (Strategy 4).

This book ends with the beginning in mind because this wraparound approach encompasses the specific best practices that some of the most successful salespeople and account managers around the world employ. At the start, we challenged you to select a customer to focus on while reading, because there's no better way to experience *Engage/Win/Grow* than with a real customer in mind.

Do you recall the question we asked in the Introduction: What percentage of the customer's total work time is spent actively buying from you? Whether the answer is a typical 1 or 2 percent or the occasional 5 percent of a highly active buyer, the reality is that your customer spends the vast majority of their time *not* buying from you. We believe that what happens during this time—call it the other 98 percent—heavily influences the small percentage of time that the customer spends in actual buying mode with you.

The world we live in is undeniably customer-driven. Today's buyers are the most educated and technologically advanced in history, and, in many cases, they are driving your sales process more than you are. Traditional sales approaches are no longer sufficient. Even if your sales performance is excellent, you can still get a grade of "incomplete" or worse when your customer is not buying, which accounts for the vast majority of their time, energy, and focus. Keeping up in the current sales environment requires more than yesterday's tools or a bag full of tips and tricks designed to control and manipulate your customer. Understanding and executing the twelve proven strategies we've presented can increase your chances for success.

Will Your *Engage/Win/Grow* Circle Be Unbroken?

Change isn't easy, and your customer's world is changing. It may even have changed while you've been reading this book. Think of it this way: you can wait for the customer-driven world to come to you, or you can up your game and take it to the customer-driven world.

We've discussed momentum and its importance in sales and account management; it keeps things moving and growing stronger over time. We hope this book has provided you with momentum, and that it helps strengthen your engagement with your customers. We also discussed actionable awareness, and we trust that you've gained some as you've discovered the 12 strategies and how top performers from around the world are deploying them before, during, and after their sales.

Finally, we've discussed value throughout this book, and we anticipate that you will realize some for yourself. If these concepts and best practices captured *your* mindshare, then put them to work. What's most important now is your commitment to engage, win, and grow. It's time to move beyond the sales process to create even more value more often with your customers.

Testing Your Effectiveness: Expand the Relationship

The following six sets of questions will help you determine your effectiveness in expanding the relationship with your customer:

1. **When you consider the concept of momentum and how it has been discussed, when and how have you experienced momentum in working with your customers?** *Do you feel that you gained as much strength and velocity as you could have? Next time, will you do anything differently when you begin to feel the force of momentum in your customer engagement?*

2. **As you consider the concepts and best practices of *Engage/ Win/Grow,* in which area do you feel that you are the strongest (before, during, or after the sale)?** *If you asked your customers to identify the areas where you could use the most improvement, what would they say? What would your colleagues say?*

3. **If we asked your customer's team members how you have helped them realize value, how would they respond?** *Do you*

think that you would be pleased with their answers? When do you plan to ask?

4. **If we asked them who achieved success as a result of this value, what do you think they would say?** *Would they be dissatisfied, satisfied, or delighted with the success that your value creation and co-creation have helped them achieve? Did you set their value expectations properly before and during the sale? Is there anything that you might do differently next time?*

5. **If we asked them why they should re-engage with you, how would their response differ from yours?** *Do you believe that they understand the past proven value that you and your organization have created and co-created with them? If so, could they articulate it? Could they extrapolate it for visioning areas of future potential value?*

6. **If we asked your customer where you could help them achieve success again, what would they say?** *Would you hear different things from different members of your customer's team? Why? Is it because they might perceive value differently?*

Case Studies

Siemens AG

Headquartered in Munich, Germany, Siemens is a global corporation with a mission to provide innovative offerings to the electrical world. Siemens operates nine divisions and is active in more than 200 countries, supporting its vast global base of customers in areas of electrification, automation and digitalization. One of the world's largest producers of energy-efficient, resource-saving technologies, Siemens is No. 1 in offshore wind turbine construction, a leading supplier of combined cycle turbines for power generation, a major provider of power transmission solutions, and a pioneer in infrastructure solutions as well as automation, drive, and software solutions for industry. The company is also a leading provider of medical imaging equipment—such as computed tomography and magnetic resonance imaging systems—and a leader in laboratory diagnostics as well as clinical IT. Siemens revenues for fiscal year 2014 were in excess of $98 billion, employing over 340,000 people across the globe.

Siemens prides itself on the technological leadership of its portfolio as demonstrated by the numerous innovations that the company has brought to market, as well as an ongoing excellence in quality and reliability. Siemens' engineers have developed many of the world's leading technologies in the automation of industrial production, medical imaging, ecofriendly production, distribution of electricity, and the transportation of people throughout the world's major cities.

In addition to bringing these, and other innovations to market, Siemens is also a B2B leader in its approach to engaging with customers, who know they can count on the company to deliver value and commit to long-term relationships that cover all levels of their organizations across the globe.

Pedro Miranda, Corporate Vice President of Siemens AG in Munich puts it this way: "Siemens considers customer proximity to be the key element of sustainable business development, enabling long-term and trust-based relationships, and coupled with the delivery of quality products, innovative systems, and reliable solutions, it's a powerful driver of continuous business success in our organization."

Customer Engagement: What Siemens Does to Effectively Engage Customers

Siemens goes to market with technically advanced products and solutions, engaging with buying centers that are frequently distributed across divisions and departments within the customer's organization. To achieve this with consistency in complex environments across the globe, Siemens has deployed an integrated approach to sales and account management, enabling stronger alignment with customers through its network of go-to-market channels. This includes not only direct sales but also Siemens' partners, which include consultants, EPCs, (Engineering, Procurement, and Construction contractors), distributors, integrators, and machine builders. Beyond that, Siemens has built a mature key account management (KAM) program, with dedicated organizations focusing on customer industries. Siemens' KAM Program has been recognized by SAMA as one of the strongest and most effective in the world.

Foremost in Siemens' approach to customer engagement is a commitment to maintain high levels of customer care across all channels, which allows consistency in engagement and customer service with strategic or "key" customers. Siemens recognized long ago that certain types of customers had the expectation that strategic suppliers would rapidly evolve beyond traditional KPI (key performance indicator) measurements (investment cost, success rate, on-time/on-budget, and time-to-delivery) to TCO (total cost of ownership), a more holistic, long-term concept that keeps suppliers engaged long after the sale is complete.

While KPI measures tend to be finalized in months or even weeks after a sale is completed, a commitment to TCO for strategic customers required Siemens to extend and expand its sales approach to a more advanced, value-selling model. This required sales and KAM processes to connect and align with the customer's business at all levels. It also required salespeople and key account managers to become more comfortable speaking the language of the customer at all levels, to get closer to the customer, and to understand and communicate how Siemens can create value for the customer, both now and into the future.

Hajo Rapp, Senior Vice President of Siemens One Customer Relationship Management, explains: "We have implemented a KAM program which is quite developed and builds on consequent customer segmentation, as well as the capabilities of our key account managers. Our internal KAM certification program supports these efforts, and we continue to strive for further improvements based on active benchmarking and ongoing support from KAM-specific research."

Engagement Excellence: How Siemens Gets It Right for Customers

As a crucial lever of its KAM program, Siemens has created organizations that are dedicated to one specific vertical market each. This helps to ensure that there is a consistent Siemens approach within each vertical market, and that all Siemens customers within a specific vertical market are served in an industry-specific manner. All KAMs within a vertical are expected to leverage the assets of their respective "center of competence" in a variety of different competency and best practice areas, including technical, commercial, legal, and marketing.

These vertical market organizations ensure customer focus throughout the Siemens organization, providing subject matter expertise, best practices, and support to the key account managers and their customer-facing team members. One critical success factor has proven to be the alignment of the respective Siemens business units via the vertical market organizations, creating synergies horizontally across Siemens and market-specific value for their customers. This approach ensures that strategies are synergized, that internal conflicts are minimized, and that customers come first before, during, and after the sale.

The Impact: Why Engagement Excellence Matters to Siemens' Customers

In the last five years, business from Siemens' KAM-managed customers grew from 40 percent to 51 percent of the company's total revenue. In parallel, Siemens also achieved increased customer satisfaction, as measured through Net Promoter scores. Siemens observed that KAM-managed customer relationships resulted in growing customer intimacy and confidence in Siemens' products and solutions, and improved Siemens' position against competitors.

Stora Enso, an industry leader in paper, bio-materials, wood products, and packaging, also felt the impact and agrees that supplier KAM programs can have a significant effect on the customer's business. Jouko Karvinin, former CEO and President of Stora Enso, offers this perspective:

> "From world class industrial technology (Siemens) to the renewable materials that will build the intelligent homes of the future (Stora Enso), a proactive, multi-level relationship between corporations in different industries (or key account management) may not be a new invention. However, in today's increasingly diverse environment, it can create totally new value for an organization, far beyond the traditional supplier/customer relationship."

The Takeaway: Why This Matters to You

Siemens rightly observes that "sales" has elements of both science and art. The "science" of sales provides insights and actionable awareness into what you know, what you offer, and how to replicate it, while the "art" requires that suppliers connect and align their solutions in ways that really matter to the customer.

Organizing customer relationships around a KAM model not only drives greater value creation and efficiencies, but also enables the supplier to view customer relationships through the lens of a long-term partnership, thus facilitating effective customer engagement.

Engelbert Schrapp, Siemens' Corporate Account Manager for Stora Enso agrees. "Excellence before, during, and after the sale requires a long term approach, which leads to continuity," he says. "Continuity creates trust and understanding, which are critical factors for success in KAM. The 'art' of KAM is then to develop new ideas and new business opportunities that go beyond classical B2B relationships. When this happens, we have evolved from a B2B relationship into a B2B partnership."

Siemens demonstrates that when an organization is firmly committed to account management and organizes customer-facing teams based on what is ultimately best for the customer, the rewards can be significant to both parties: before, during, and long after the sale.

Hilton Worldwide

Hilton Worldwide is one of the largest and most successful hospitality companies in the world. The Hilton story began in 1919, when Conrad Hilton opened his first forty-room hotel in a small Texas town. Now based in McLean, Virginia, Hilton Worldwide has grown to oversee twelve brands, more than 4,200 hotels, and 699,000 rooms, operating in twenty-four time zones and ninety-three countries. Hilton brands have become a beacon for innovation, quality, and success across the globe.

Hilton Worldwide has also developed a reputation for excellence with its premier strategic business customers. After years of interaction and growth with what some viewed as the "perfect customer," Hilton wisely concluded that building collaborative, mutually beneficial relationships led to value co-creation and improved business productivity for both parties. Danny Hughes, Senior Vice President of Sales and Revenue Management for Americas at Hilton Worldwide, put it this way:

> "As one of the world's leading hospitality organizations, we've learned much about taking care of our customers over the past 95 years. But when it comes to our most strategic global accounts, we have fully embraced the concept of partnering. The value that we are creating together with these customers is impressive, and the results from our investment in these partnerships are significant."

Customer Engagement: What Hilton Does to Effectively Engage Customers

After experiencing the benefits of customer relationships based on mutual value creation, Hilton began a journey in 2004 to become an early adopter and leader in the field of strategic account management (SAM). Leveraging the knowledge and resources provided by the Strategic Account Management Association (SAMA), the company launched its own SAM program in January 2005. Hilton began by hiring and training five global account directors and identifying fifteen accounts that were considered strategic to their business. The new global account director role was defined as the "leader and guardian" of the global, enterprise-wide strategy for each of their assigned strategic accounts, and their responsibilities included the following:

- Facilitation of cross-functional teams to create account business plans for each customer.

- Alignment of resources and team responsibilities in support of the customer and customer strategy.

- Positioning of Hilton Worldwide through one global "voice to the customer."

- Differentiation of the value of doing business with Hilton.

The first year of SAM at Hilton was largely devoted to discovery, uncovering common synergies, building and growing trust-based relationships, and filling the pipeline with new opportunities. Leadership understood that the first year was one of "development," so program success metrics focused on establishing internal and external relationships, quantity/quality of needs assessments completed, opportunities developed or discovered to "make and save money" for both companies, opportunities brought to fruition, and customer satisfaction and loyalty survey ratings. Accountability for business growth began in 2006 when success metrics were defined, including year-over-year revenue growth, growth of market share, and "make and save money" initiatives brought to fruition. Hilton also monitored both the quality and level of customer engagement and continued to evaluate customer satisfaction and loyalty survey ratings.

Hilton acknowledges that the first few years of building a strategic/global accounts program are the most challenging. Executive support and sponsorship took time to develop, and enterprise-wide visibility was low. But despite obstacles, the Hilton SAM team persevered; the newly developed strategy started showing results at a pace that more than satisfied leadership. Perhaps just as important, lessons were learned that influenced the evolution of Hilton's SAM program as it now exists. Today, Hilton's expanded team of global account directors manages and grows the strategic relationships between Hilton Worldwide and fifty of the world's leading companies.

In 2013, SAMA selected Hilton Worldwide to receive its prestigious *Program of the Year* award, specifically recognizing Hilton's account management efforts in the following areas:

- **Process:** embedded for execution.

- **People:** talent selection and development.

- **Leadership:** branding the SAM Program.

- **Sustainable Program:** growth through transformation.

- **Performance:** mutual results and outcomes.

Denise Lodrige-Kover, Vice President of Global Strategic Account Management, now retired, who guided Hilton's account management efforts from inception, offers this perspective:

> "Our commitment from the beginning of our journey has been to superior relationship management. SAM represents trusted advisor relationships, innovative solution delivery, and market share domination. Through frequent engagement, collaboration, and executing an approach that focuses on mutual outcomes, SAM has been successful in optimizing business and achieving the highest customer loyalty to Hilton Worldwide."

Engagement Excellence: How Hilton Gets It Right for Customers

When large suppliers engage with large customers, it's often difficult to navigate through both organizations and make the right connections between the two companies. When this occurs, the resulting problems can include a mutual lack of understanding, limited visibility into each other's organization, and the development of a "silo-to-silo" environment, making it virtually impossible for customer and supplier to align their strategic business objectives.

With a mature SAM program in place today, Hilton Worldwide is now able to overcome such challenges and create "partner-to-partner" relationships with strategic customers. The company is now capable of deploying cross-functional teams on a global basis to align and connect with strategic customers' teams, growing relationships while avoiding silo pitfalls. A cross-functional team can consist of global team members from various Hilton business units who are aligned with the customer to manage and grow relationships on global, national, and regional levels. Hilton provides global advocacy for strategic customers and their account management best practices today are the direct result of an ongoing commitment to invest in their people through recognition, rewards, and training. Hilton has established a strong internal communication plan to share achievements, recognize successes, and drive transparency throughout the organization regarding the impact of the SAM program.

Hilton also provides customer-specific value propositions to strategic accounts by delivering targeted solutions that address specific challenges and business objectives. By providing account managers who serve as trusted advisors to their customers, Hilton has been able to successfully elevate strategic customer relationships into partnerships, giving rise to value creation and co-creation, resulting in new opportunities to share and implement best practices. Hilton's excellent customer engagement includes finding common synergies with customers that enable both organizations to collaborate and align. When this happens, Hilton is able to engage with customers at higher levels, deliver more value through enterprise-wide proposals, and as the results have shown, ultimately increase revenues and market share.

The Impact: Why Engagement Excellence Matters to Hilton's Customers

Although it can take 5 to 8 years to develop a mature SAM program, Hilton Worldwide experienced benefits and a positive impact on their business fairly quickly. Within 2 years of launch, they achieved a 20 percent premium growth above market conditions in their SAM accounts. Within 3 years, market share increase in all of their SAM accounts exceeded expectations, double-digit growth continued, and customer satisfaction was approaching the 90th percentile. Within the first 4 years, the revenue from the original accounts grew over 100 percent, revenue and market share growth continued in all SAM accounts, and customer satisfaction reached well beyond the 90th percentile.

Today, the revenues managed through the Hilton SAM program have expanded to well over $1.5 billion annually. Most importantly, value and growth are delivered to both Hilton and the customer as a result of this commitment to customer engagement excellence, as proclaimed through the most important voices of all: Hilton's customers. A recent customer satisfaction and loyalty survey rates the impact of Hilton's SAM program at 95 to 99 percent overall satisfaction. Hilton has achieved trusted advisor status with many of its strategic accounts, a relational level that not only positions Hilton to create and co-create ongoing mutual value with these customers, but also results in more engaging, productive, and rewarding work environments for both parties.

Procter and Gamble (P&G), a leading multinational consumer goods company, has also experienced the impact of Hilton's commitment to excellent customer engagement. Alan Tomblin, P&G's North American Sales Manager, has this to say:

> "Here at P&G, we have experienced the impact of Hilton's investment in 'superior relationship management' and its value is felt by our organization and in our business relationship with this world-class company. But to make this happen requires the right people and the right business processes, and Hilton's approach to customer engagement and the people that lead these efforts make a significant difference in our relationship."

The Takeaway: Why This Matters to You

The Hilton Worldwide journey is an outstanding example of a world-class approach to account management. By building collaborative, mutually beneficial relationships with its premier clients, Hilton continues to develop long-term B2B partnerships with them, resulting in mutual business growth that is supported by increases in productivity, revenues, and customer loyalty.

Keith Hymel, Hilton's Senior Director of Global Accounts, who is responsible for Hilton's business with P&G, offers this perspective:

> "Our partnership with P&G extends across multiple business units and levels within both organizations, and this has positioned us to drive value creation to areas that simply wouldn't have been possible otherwise. But underneath this are authentic, trust-based relationships, and this is the foundation that enables the communication and collaboration that ultimately leads to this value."

Hilton's unwavering commitment to continually grow and improve its SAM program has ultimately resulted in measurable outcomes that include stronger customer relationships and the creation and co-creation of mutual value. Overall, the Hilton example demonstrates that a well-executed SAM program benefits both the customer and the supplier before, during, and after the sale.

Securian Financial Group—Group Insurance

Securian Financial Group, Inc. and its affiliates provide high-quality financial security solutions to meet a variety of client needs, offering financial security to more than 15 million people nationwide through insurance, investment, and retirement products. As of 2014, Securian's life insurance company affiliates—Minnesota Life and Securian Life—had more than $1 trillion of life insurance in force.

Securian's Group Insurance division offers financial protection to millions of people through employers across the country. For over 80 years the division has provided customized group insurance solutions to meet the benefit needs of its employer customers. The division's value proposition of excellent service and innovative technology aims to make it easy for employers to deliver competitive insurance benefits that attract and retain employees.

According to data from SNL Financial LC, from 2010 to 2014, Securian's Group Insurance division had a client retention rate of 97 percent. The division also has high associate retention—in 2015, its twenty-nine account team members had an average 18 years of service—so customers benefit from the expertise offered by tenured and highly educated account teams. This has contributed directly to the division's rapid growth: Securian, according to SNL Financial LC data, was the nation's third largest direct writer of group life insurance by 2013. Fifteen years prior, it was barely in the top twenty.

Securian's Group Insurance leaders attribute the division's exceptional success with its strategic employer customers to a focus on guiding business principles and core values that include trust, strength, integrity, quality, and respect. Von Peterson, Securian's Senior Vice President of Group Insurance, adds this perspective:

> "We never take anything for granted—our business, our relationships, or the privilege we have in working with customers. We know our customers have choices, and we view ourselves as stewards of their business. We are responsible for diligent and prudent management

of what they have entrusted to us. In short, we treat our customers as we would want to be treated."

Customer Engagement: What Securian Does to Effectively Engage Customers

The Securian Group Insurance division's stewardship approach has earned the company an outstanding reputation as a customer-centric organization. Demonstrating their firm commitment to customer relationships, Kristi Fox, Second Vice President of Group Client Relationships, highlights the importance of effective customer engagement:

> "We take this approach very seriously, and we refer to our customer meetings as 'stewardship meetings.' When we engage with customers, it's an opportunity to sit down together to focus on their insurance plans, to let clients know how their plan is doing financially, and to discuss participation in the plan and our service to them and their employees. We talk about the future. It's important that we understand our clients' business, global benefit initiatives, and upcoming short-term and long-term priorities. We stay focused on those things that the customer truly values, and ensure that they leave these meetings more informed than when they arrived."

To achieve this, the division emphasizes educating and developing its customer-facing teams. Because the insurance business is data-intensive, account team members are thoroughly trained to understand the data, and more importantly, the story behind it. Fox adds:

> "We recognize that our customers must make sense of a tremendous amount of sensitive and complex information, and then communicate that information to their own organizations so they can make sound business decisions. Our training and service approach is highly focused on helping customers understand and learn how to utilize

data to tell the story within their own organizations. We don't just rely on sending them a written report—we help our customers connect the dots; we educate. That's where the unique value resides."

Engagement Excellence: How Securian Gets It Right for Customers

The Securian Group Insurance division's excellence in customer engagement is not just limited to providing valuable information in customer meetings, but also extends to a full suite of technology-enabled services developed first for the customer and secondarily for Securian. An early example is the development of online beneficiary management that allowed employees themselves to designate beneficiaries online, freeing the employer to focus on the core elements of their business.

Operating in an industry that many would describe as complex, Securian's Group Insurance division recognizes that transparency and simplicity are key to developing long-lasting relationships. This is what their customers need and depend on, whether they articulate it or not.

Long before technology began to drive the industry, Securian recognized that the insurance purchasing and administration processes include tasks that could be cumbersome to customers. The division approached this industry-wide concern as an opportunity to simplify, streamline, innovate, create value, and ultimately gain advantage over competitors. After listening carefully to their customers' feedback, Securian developed new technology that enabled representatives from customer organizations to query the status of their employees' applications for coverage. The technology provided immediate transparency for end-users, who were now also able to obtain relevant information about requirements from the initial application through approval. Providing fast and easy access to ongoing developments, Securian's customer accessible technology became a huge hit. Both Securian and its customers saved time, and were better informed and equipped to respond to questions that employees inevitably ask during the application process. Securian continued to break ground in developing new technologies in the years that followed. They recognized that they were judged against best-of-breed in technology not only inside the group insurance industry, but outside as well.

While most of the advancements and processes were designed with customers in mind, Securian's Group Insurance division leadership found that the benefit also extended to Securian. Von Peterson notes:

> "We didn't immediately recognize the 'win-win' magnitude when we first developed these new customer-focused technologies and services. But time after time, they've worked in everybody's favor. The best kind of meeting is one where a customer tells us about a problem they are having that seems unsolvable. By really listening to our customer's concerns, we can identify the source of their challenges, and can develop a solution or capability that responds appropriately. The result not only benefits the customer we're responding to, but it also enhances what we offer to other existing customers and potential new ones. As our relationships with customers grow stronger and deeper, we become stronger and more capable of delivering on our value proposition."

The Impact: Why Engagement Excellence Matters to Securian's Customers

Through a customer-focused approach, Securian's Group Insurance division continues to solidify its reputation as an industry leader. By listening to customers and developing innovative solutions, Securian's relationships with key strategic customers and leading companies across the country have been elevated to trusted advisor status. This is evidenced by the division's 2013 and 2015 Net Promoter scores of 89 and 88, respectively, which indicate that Securian's Group Insurance customers are very willing to recommend the company to others.

One of Securian's strategic employer customers gives insight: "We've found Securian to be unique in the industry," says Denise Murphy, Director of Benefits and Wellness at the University of Notre Dame. "For the past 12 years, they've been consistently high-service, focusing on our needs first and always looking for innovative ways to provide access to what we need quickly and efficiently. This makes us more effective in what we can do for our faculty and staff, and it's why we genuinely value our relationship with Securian."

Securian Manager of Client Relationships, Laura Lundquist, who has worked with Notre Dame for over a decade, adds: "Our success with our customer correlates directly with our stewardship approach. Whether it's with an existing relationship, or a potential new customer, our planning is very deliberate. We continually seek ways to innovate and add value. I have no doubt this long-term, collaborative approach creates more wins for everyone involved."

The Takeaway: Why This Matters to You

The Securian Group Insurance division's stewardship approach is deeply embedded in the company's culture and extends out to its affiliates. The organization exemplifies what can happen when emphasis is placed on ongoing training and retention of internal staff, who can in turn educate customers and use what they know to simplify a data-intensive and complex business. Securian continues to innovate and pursue first-to-market solutions that respond directly to customer feedback. With its customer engagement bar set very high, and a philosophy that embraces stewardship, Securian is likely to continue to achieve success before, during, and after the sale.

Afterword

BEYOND THE SALES PROCESS was written for sales and customer facing professionals, and their managers and leaders. We framed your *Engage/Win/Grow* journey in three parts to bring clarity and understanding to how you can go beyond the sales process before, during, and after your sales.

Working with the organizations and their customers that agreed to be featured in this book, our objective has been to provide you with proven strategies and real examples of how some of the best-of-the-best engage differently. Regardless of your industry, solutions, products, or markets, we urge you to consider the common elements that run through all of the case studies. In each one, a salesperson or an account manager engages, wins, and grows effectively with the customer to create and co-create value; a customer realizes and validates value as a result; and salespeople and account managers go beyond the sales process by implementing and embracing twelve proven strategies for their customer-driven world.

This book provides you with an approach that will equip you for sales success today and tomorrow. We hope you will put it to use, and we wish you good fortune in your journey before, during, and after your next sale.

For updates, insights, and other relevant information, please visit the authors at BeyondTheSalesProcess.com.

Index

About the Authors

STEVE ANDERSEN founded Performance Methods, Inc. (PMI) following a successful 20-year technology career that included multiple appointments as chief sales officer. PMI's unique approach provides clients with customized sales, account management, and sales management solutions that are among the most highly regarded within the sales performance industry. Steve's background includes extensive experience in sales, sales management, and sales leadership, and he brings a contemporary, practical view to his work with clients, which include many of the world's largest corporations. Steve has addressed a variety of audiences on a wide range of sales and account management topics, and has published numerous articles in the areas of sales, sales management, and account management best practices.

DAVE STEIN has worked as a sales representative, sales manager, Director of Worldwide Sales Development, VP of Sales, VP of International Operations, VP of Client Services, sales strategist, and consultant. His hands-on work with businesses ranging from start-ups to the Global 100 provides him with a unique and pragmatic view of sales methodologies, sales training approaches, social selling, and the cultural, behavioral, and operational changes required for corporations to excel at the sales function. Dave's first book, *How Winners Sell,* was a highly-acclaimed commercial success, and he is considered an expert by *Sales & Marketing Management, Fast Company, The New York Times, BusinessWeek, Inc., Fortune, The Wall Street Journal, Harvard Business Review,* and *Forbes.*